Every Muslim Child Matters

ctical guidance for schools and children's services

Every Muslim Child Matters
practical guidance for schools and children's services

Maurice Irfan Coles

Trentham Books
Stoke on Trent, UK and Sterling, USA

Trentham Books Limited
Westview House   22883 Quicksilver Drive
734 London Road   Sterling
Oakhill   VA 20166-2012
Stoke on Trent   USA
Staffordshire
England ST4 5NP

© 2008 Maurice Irfan Coles

First published 2008

British Library Cataloguing-in-Publication Data
A catalogue record for this book is available from the
British Library

ISBN: 978 1 85856 421 0

Cover: Blue Mosque in Istanbul.

Designed and typeset by Trentham Print Design Ltd., Chester and printed in Great Britain by Cromwell Press Ltd, Wiltshire.

Contents

Introduction

This book sets out to be both ambitious and innovative. It is ambitious because it covers the major issues that young British Muslims face today. It seeks to demonstrate that the Islamic faith is the key determinant in the lives of Muslim children and young people, and that all services involved in their education, health and social care must take this perspective on board if they are to meet pupil need.

It is innovative because it maps the Islamic perspective against the five outcomes of Every Child Matters and offers a commentary to support schools, children's services and their many partners. It builds upon much of the earlier work undertaken by the SDSA on Islam and the curriculum but places this within the new QCA framework for Key Stages 3 and 4, and within the new curriculum agenda that is ideally suited to address so many of the issues raised. Each section can be read as a stand-alone but readers are advised to read the new strategy first because the perspectives outlined inform everything that follows.

The book is very much a School Development Support Agency (SDSA) team effort, and exemplifies the spirit of open discourse, collaboration and shared values that characterise the agency. It originated in a presentation made to the first Inter-LEA conference specifically designed to address issues related to Islam and Education, organised jointly by Leicester City's SDSA and the University of Leicester in February 2003 (www.sdsa.net). This, in turn, led to a widely circulated article, a number of educational publications and a major research project for the DfES which was designed to identify the National Curriculum potential to reflect the experiences of pupils of Muslim and African-Caribbean origin, which became known as the CREAM project. The DfES use of the term 'Muslim', as opposed to an ethnic grouping like Pakistani or Bangladeshi was, in itself, brave and innovative because it presupposed that faith was a key determinant, if not *the* key determinant of Muslim identity regardless of cultural or ethnic background. It also led to what Hugh Edwards in News at Ten on BBC television described as 'a pioneering conference', at which 120 young British Muslims were brought together to discuss issues that were relevant to them. Their perceptions, concerns and insights inform much of the thinking that permeates this work.

At that time the author entered uncharted territory for Local Education Authorities (LEAs) with great humility and even greater trepidation, conscious that, although a Muslim convert, a practising *Naqsbandi* Sufi and a Senior Education Officer with a lifetime spent dealing with race, faith and cohesion issues, he had no background of Islamic scholarship. He was equally conscious that there were likely to be Muslims who would question some of the basic tenets of the argument, and some LEAs and schools who would prefer to leave well alone for fear of arousing even greater passions. Since then the educational and political landscapes have changed beyond recognition and the work that began in earnest in 2003 now has a greater imperative and resonance than ever. Issues of Islam and its place in schools, in British and European society, and globally have to be addressed if we are to achieve the just, cohesive and harmonious society we espouse.

Sincere thanks are due to Mick Waters, QCA's Director of Curriculum who has been supportive throughout and who has kindly permitted use of QCA material; and great thanks are due to all members of the SDSA team. Robert Vincent, who has supported the Inter-LEA conferences from their inception, reviewed the writing, challenged the thinking and has contributed enormously to the community cohesion and data analysis perspectives, in which he is an acknowledged expert. Pete Chilvers was the key player in the CREAM research and in the development of '*Education in Islam: Developing a Culturally Inclusive Curriculum*' (www.sdsa.net) and many of Pete's educational insights appear in this volume, amended and updated but pedagogically sound. Alan Curtis, who has been instrumental in developing Student Voice and who was in part responsible for the ground breaking Young British Muslim Conference and Khalid Mahmood, whose passion and drive in the field of supplementary education has pioneered the developmental work of mainstream schools and madrasahs in unprecedented collaboration. The whole team have made their mark in this book. Even the SDSA's latest recruit, Julia Leith (Complementary Schools Project Delivery Officer and Director of Leading Edge) has significantly contributed to the Modern Languages paragraph. Robert Bunting, our consultant for several of our projects, kindly offered his expertise and wisdom in writing the chapter on Islam and the arts. Books maybe written by academics and authors but they would never see the light of day without administrative support. Great thanks are due to Shaaeda Qureshi for her perseverance, patience and enormous efficiency in typing the text, commenting on its accuracy and supporting the research; and to Lara Coles for her painstaking work on revising the text and completing the indexing and bibliographies. Finally, special tribute must be paid to the SDSA's Operations Manager, Cas Beckett, without whose iron discipline and constant nagging, this book would never have been finished.

I end, in a spirit of humility, with praise for my own Shaykh, Mohammed Rashid, who has been a constant source of inspiration, and to Shaykh Ibrahim Mogra (MCB) whose critical thinking, work and moderation I value so highly and who kindly read and commented on the material. Finally, in keeping with the traditions and spirit of Islam, all praise must go to God who started me on this journey and to whom everything is owed.

Maurice Irfan Coles
April 2008

1

Every Muslim Child Matters:
Towards a new strategic approach

This chapter invites frank, open and honest discourse about the nature of Islam in Britain today and the responsibility and contribution schools, Children and Young People's Services and their partners can make to help shape the debate. It considerably widens the traditional debate that has largely centred upon the levels of attainment (or more precisely, under-attainment) of the two largest Muslim communities, Pakistani/Kashmiri and Bangladeshi; and on meeting the religious and cultural needs of Muslim pupils. In particular, it addresses issues related to the education of British Muslims within a Muslim frame of reference. Further, given that Muslims, particularly boys, spend so much time in madrasahs, it seeks to encourage potential synergies between the maintained supplementary/complementary sectors of education. Finally, it locates the whole discourse firmly within wider multicultural, multi-faith, race equality perspectives and aims to justify and suggest a strategic approach to addressing the educational issues of community cohesion as they relate to the Muslim communities.

When a suicide bomber cries '*Allahu akbar*' in their final act of killing innocents, the majority of the 1.6 million Muslims in the UK wonder whether this is the same Allah to whom they pray five times a day and with whom they try to be in constant remembrance. The great majority of British Muslims, in so far as they understand the rationale behind suicide bombings at all, believe that it is based upon a hideous distortion of one of the world's great religions, one of the world's great civilisations. Barely a day passes without some press reference – invariably negative but sometimes positive – to Islam and its place in the west. Paradoxically, the frightening litany of suicide bombings and negative perceptions of Muslims has to be set against what a recent Department of Local Government and Communities report has called a 're-surgence of confidence amongst all faith groups' in the UK and a 'renaissance of recognition that these groups have a major role to play in promotion of the community cohesion in most areas of our civic and public life' (Coles *et al*, 2006). This resurgence of confidence is particularly true of the Muslim communities, especially amongst the young who are becoming increasingly vocal about their place as British citizens. It is against this background of confidence and of killing that this opening chapter is set.

Since the opening conference in 2003 that launched the LEA's drive to meet the needs of Muslim pupils more effectively, the educational and political landscapes have changed almost beyond recognition.

Local Education Authorities have been replaced by Local Authorities (LAs) and their Children and Young People's Services (CYPS) combining, as they do, the old LEA functions with those of social services that were targeted on 0-19 provision. Similarly, the Department for Education and Skills has been re-designated and restructured as the Department for Children, Schools and Families (DCSF) which is responsible for children's services, the curriculum, families, schools, 14-19 education, and the Respect Taskforce. In addition, the DCSF is responsible for inputting into the Government's strategy for ending child poverty, with the Department of Work and Pensions and into promoting the health of all children by working with, for example, the Department of Culture, Media and Sport. Although curriculum and assessment advice remains with the Qualifications and Curriculum Authority (QCA) even here there has been a quiet revolution since 2003, with the gradual freeing of the curriculum from its earlier centralised prescription and a keener appreciation of the implications of the personalised learning agenda. There is also a new Department of Innovation, Universities and Skills (DIUS) aimed at expanding high-end graduate skills and raising the skills of the wider adult workforce. This Department takes responsibility from the Department of Trade and Industry for making Britain 'one of the best places in the world for science, research and innovation'. In addition, in May 2006 the department for Communities and Local Government was created (CLG) to help build the capacity of communities, to promote cohesion and to tackle extremism.

The CLG was created in part because the wider political landscape too has changed. The tragic and evil acts of September 2001 were savagely brought home to mainland Britain on July 7 2005 with the London suicide bombings. Britain woke up to the harsh realities that these bombers were not, unlike those of 9/11 in the US, foreign terrorist but were home grown, the products of a British educational system and members of British Muslim communities. Since 7/7 there have been several cases of thwarted bomb attempts, the most high profile of which took place in London and Glasgow in late June 2007 and culminated in the arrest of an Iraqi born doctor. Each of these outrages fuels the rise of Islamophobia, and adds to the tension and general soul searching within our Muslim communities. Extremist acts have given an even greater sense of urgency to the debate about what it means to be a British Muslim. After wide consultation the Government, supported by members of the Muslim community launched its strategy, *'Preventing Violent Extremism – Winning Hearts and Minds'* (Communities and Local Government April, 2007). For Government the challenge is clear:

> This is not about a clash of civilizations or a struggle between Islam and 'the West.' It is about standing up to a small fringe of terrorists and their extremist supporters. Indeed, Government is committed to working in partnership with the vast majority of Muslims who reject violence and who share core British values in doing this

Muslims share and can sign up to the British core values which are non-negotiable: 'respect for the rule of law, freedom of speech, equality of opportunity, respect for others and responsibility for others' (CLG April, 2007). The major problem is that violent extremists can successfully exploit the lack of understanding of Islam. Sir Keith Ajegbo's *Diversity and Citizenship Review* (2007) addressed Islam as part of a broader understanding of the issues of diversity and identity in the UK and with the DCSF is exploring ways in which faith and cultural issues can be addressed more effectively through the national curriculum. And the issues are not limited to school aged pupils. The Further and Higher Education sectors can provide even more fertile places for those attracted to extremist ideologies. Both sectors are exploring ways in which they can broaden faith understanding. In Higher Education Dr. Siddiqui's important report to the DfES (May 2007) was explicitly critical of the present state of Islamic studies in many universities, which he found predominantly grounded in the needs of diplomacy and foreign affairs: a colonial legacy. His research echoed the views of young people in schools explored by Coles *et al*, in that 'the young Muslims in this country and in Europe are looking to express Islam in a context that their parents' generation can hardly have experienced, namely living in a modern secular culture grounded in Judaeo-Christian traditions.' Siddiqui recommended that Islamic studies should focus on the theological and civilisational aspects of Islam relevant to the contemporary practices of the faith.

These evolving political and educational landscapes and the structural changes that have followed at local and national level will have a profound impact on Muslim issues and Muslim people's life chances. This is particularly true for all the services dealing with children and young people. For these services, the greatest driver for change and the yardstick against which they will be measured is the five outcomes of the *Every Child Matters (ECM): Change for Children Agenda*, (DfES 2004), accompanied as it now is with *Every Parent Matters* (DfES 2007). ECM is a radically new approach to the wellbeing of children and young people from birth to age 19, which aims is to ensure that every child, whatever their background or their circumstances, has the support they need to:

- be healthy
- stay safe
- enjoy and achieve
- make a positive contribution
- achieve economic wellbeing

This means that the organisations involved with providing services to children – from hospitals and schools to police and voluntary groups – have teamed up in new ways, sharing information and working together, in order to protect children from harm and help them achieve throughout life. Central to effective ECM implementation is that young people will have far more say about issues that affect them as individuals and collectively.

Much of the original impetus for *Every Child Matters* came from some high profile cases involving system failures in dealing with seriously abused children. In 2003 the government published a green paper, *Every Child Matters*, alongside its formal response to the report into the death of Victoria Climbié, the young girl who was horrifically abused, tortured and killed by her great aunt and the man with whom they lived. The focus of the green paper was very much on supporting families and carers, ensuring early intervention and improving service integration. Subsequent debate and legislation considerably widened the early focus so that the ever increasing range of personnel involved in the children's workforce is directly involved in securing the outcomes.

The Government's view is essentially holistic. Concentrating exclusively on schools to raise attainment, especially for those from less socially and economically advantaged backgrounds, might well lead to improvements in outcomes and improvements in the quality of teaching and learning, but this is unlikely to be sufficient. The safety, the health and wellbeing of all children is critical to their readiness to learn, to their overall life chances and in particular to their ability to secure their longer term economic wellbeing. ECM is, of course, by definition directed at all children but it is particularly aimed at the most disadvantaged groups in order to provide them with a better start in life. A whole range of different indicators are employed as baseline assessments which in turn lead to targeted interventions. Muslim communities generally feature very highly on all these indicators.

British Muslims: some facts

Governments need hard facts upon which to base their interventionist policies and practices. A plethora of information about Muslims now exists in practically every area of life. It is upon much of this information that many arguments in this book are based. These facts can still be a little confusing, however, in that much, but not all, of the information is collected on a faith basis. Some, like that collected by the DCSF, is entirely based upon ethnicity, and much of the other evidence we have is also broken down in this way. Generally, this is not problematic as it is relatively safe to assume faith on the basis of ethnic grouping, as by far the majority of Pakistanis, Bangladeshis, Turks and Somalis are likely to be Muslim.

The overriding conclusions are stark: generally Muslims are the most religious, and the most likely to live in family households. They are also the poorest, the least well educated, the least likely to be employed, and the most likely to suffer poor health. They are now also greatly over-represented in the prison population. Great care must be taken not to assume that these characteristics of disadvantage are common to all Muslims. At the same time there is a large and increasingly vibrant, self confident and articulate group of Muslims in the professional and managerial classes who succeed as well as any other community. As the following figures on page 6/7 demonstrate, there are nonetheless major areas of disadvantage which require action.

The situation is disturbing. Other groups, in particular the white working class and children of African-Caribbean heritage suffer many of these disadvantages but the Muslim communities in Britain, especially children and young people, have the added complication of living their faith in a world which is predominantly secular, and in a world in which a few supposed adherents are hell bent on achieving their aims through the most violent and evil of means. What is required is unprecedented collaboration between all those for whom the interests of children are paramount, whether they be parents, schools, children's services, or religious institutions. The five out-

Demographics

■ There are in excess of 1.6 million Muslims in the UK. They are largely of South Asian origin (Pakistani/Kashmiri and Bangladeshi) but there are also significant numbers of Turkish, Kurdish, Somali, Yemeni and Indian origin

■ There are an increasing number of converts to Islam from within the white, African-Caribbean and mixed heritage groups

■ Muslims tend to be concentrated in London, Leicester, Luton, Leeds, Oldham, Bradford and Birmingham, with over a third in the London region

■ About 70 per cent are British born

■ About a third are under the age of 16 *(Source: National Statistics on-line)*

Faith and citizenship

■ The huge majority of Muslims polled feel that Islam is the most important thing in their lives *(Source: Coles et al, 2006)*

■ It is estimated that the majority of those aged from 4 to 14 attend madrasahs after school

■ The Gallup Organisation poll revealed 'Muslims as model citizens' *(Source: The Times 17/04/07)*

Education

■ In 2001 there were 371,000 school aged (5 – 16) Muslim children in England *(Source: www.statistics.org)*

■ Asian pupils appear to have the most positive attitudes to school, work and lessons *(Source: DfES 2006)* and have very low rates of exclusion

■ Pakistani and Bangladeshi origin pupils have constantly performed below the average for all pupils on every scale of the Foundation Stage profile *(Source: DfES 2006)*

■ Pakistani and Bangladeshi origin pupils consistently have lower levels of attainment than most other ethnic groups across all key stages *(Source: DfES 2006)* and make less progress at primary school

■ 31 per cent of young British Muslims leave school with no qualifications compared to 15 per cent of the total population *(Source: National Statistics)*

Crime

- Muslims are heavily overrepresented in prisons. They make up almost 10 per cent of the prison population, compared to 3 per cent of the total population. Two thirds are young men aged 18-30 and although there are fewer women their number has increased year on year. The Muslim population has doubled over the previous decade. About 25 per cent are incarcerated for drug related offences (Source: Prison Service Statistics, 2004 and ICC 2007)

- Muslims have the highest rates of risk of being a victim of racially motivated crime (Source: National Statistics)

- 47 per cent of Muslim students have experienced Islamophobia (Source FOSIS survey 2005)

- Between 2001 – 2003 there was a 302 per cent increase in stop and search incidents among Asian people compared with 118 per cent among white people *(Source: Home Office)*

Poverty

- 35 per cent of Muslim households have no adults in employment (more than double the national average) *(Source: Muslim Housing Experience, Oxford Centre for Islamic Studies)*

- Just under 75 per cent of Bangladeshi and Pakistani children are living in households below the poverty line *(Source: Department for Work and Pensions)*

- Many live in large households

Health

- Muslims have the highest rates of reported ill health and high rates of incidence of Special Educational Needs *(Sources: National Statistics and DfES)*

Employment

- In 2004, 28 per cent of 16-24 year old Muslims were unemployed *(Source: National Statistics)*

- In 2004, a fifth of Muslims were self-employed *(Source: National Statistics)*

- In 2004, 69 per cent of Muslim women were economically inactive *(Source: Social Trends No 36, 2006)* comes: be healthy, stay safe, make a positive contribution and achieve economic wellbeing, provide the starting point for *Every Muslim Child Matters* as they do for all communities, but the issues facing British Muslims are different in kind and in degree and go to the heart of what it means to be a Muslim in the UK in particular, and in the world in general. There are fifteen global, national and local drivers which resonate within the UK context and provide an overwhelming case for devising an overarching strategic approach for meeting the needs of Muslim pupils.

The fifteen drivers of a strategic approach to Islam and education

1   the evil and tragic events of September 11 2001 and July 7 2005 and their continuing aftermath have placed the nature of Islam itself, and the position of its adherents who are citizens of western countries, at the forefront of the agenda of many governments

2   faith and the remembrance of God, specifically through a commitment to the teaching of the Messenger Muhammad (PBUH), are the key determinants in the lives of most Muslims. A system of education and care that fails to recognise, acknowledge and build upon this is failing its young people

3.   the Muslim views of learning and of 'revealed' and 'acquired' knowledge, and of parenting and 'moral virtues' are not understood and utilised positively by schools and Children's Services

4   the omission of Muslim perspectives and of genuine recognition of Islamic civilisation from the school curriculum serves to undermine the confidence of Muslim pupils, and miseducates non-Muslims by implicitly denying the shared histories and narratives that make up pluralist Britain

5   the serious under-attainment of many Muslim pupils, particularly those of Pakistani/Kashmiri and Bangladeshi heritage, requires closer scrutiny and concerted action to close the attainment gap

6   a robust, frank and open debate about what it means to be a British Muslim is required. This debate should explore the relationship of Islam to citizenship education and will help British Muslim girls and boys in their own attempts to define their identity (ies) in Britain in the 21st century

7   this debate must take place not only in mainstream schools but also in mosques and madrasahs for the mutual benefit of both. It will help raise pupil attainment in mainstream, and support attempts madrasahs may wish to make in changing their pedagogic style and content

8   the incorporation of a Muslim frame of reference into relevant policies and practices will support schools and LAs in fulfilling their statutory requirements under the Race Relations Amendment Act (2000), and the Education Act (2006), and help them to demonstrate active implementation of their 'positive statutory duties' to promote race relations and community cohesion

9   effective responses to meeting the needs of Muslim pupils, especially when set beside the five outcomes of *Every Child Matters*, will not only help raise Muslim standards of achievement and attainment but will help to address some of the care, health and safety issues that hinder Muslim progress. It will also support school in effectively completing their Self Evaluation Form (SEF), especially if they have proactively involved parents and pupils. Similarly, their responses should satisfy some of the requirements outlined in the Ofsted framework and in the Joint Area Reviews that Local Authorities undergo

10 a strategic approach which is joined up and coherent across the range of national and local government departments will help support the drive for community cohesion, help put an end to the parallel lives and segregation of various communities and contribute to the defeat of extremism and terrorism

11 the well documented rise and rise of Islamophobia provides the even greater urgency of addressing these issues

12 the rise of Muslim extremism and sectarianism must be addressed openly so that all sectors of society, Muslim and non-Muslim, can engage with them

13 for the Muslim communities, known collectively as the *ummah*, major geo-political issues like the Israel-Palestine conflict, the disputes in Kashmir, the religious strife in Gujarat, and the presence of non-Muslim armies in Iraq and Afghanistan are very real and exist here and now; not merely for the Muslim population but also for such groups as British born Jews, those of Hindu Gujarati origin, and Punjabi Sikhs

14 many asylum seekers are of Muslim origin and can suffer the double impact of being despised for seeking asylum and for being Muslim

15 the combination of all these factors has the potential to be the explosive spark that can undermine the very roots of our shared multifaith, multicultural, multiethnic, pluralist democracy. The very complexity neces-

sitates a well thought out, clearly articulated strategy at school, Local Authority and national level

The rationale expanded

The destruction of the Twin Towers in 2001 and its global aftermath forever ended any complacency that the Western world may have had about the place of Islam in the 21st century. It brought home to Muslims and non-Muslims alike the urgency of a proper debate about what it means to be a contemporary Muslim in Britain and the world. The equally evil London bombings added a horrific sense of urgency to the British context. Arguments have raged about the antecedents of such horrific deeds with a range of scholars attempting to discover how and why such acts have been committed. This analysis is often complex and historically far-reaching and appears to have its roots in the decline of Islam as a global power.

To many Muslims, who do not distinguish between political power and that based upon religion and spirit, such a decline is inexplicable. As Abdelwahab Meddeb eloquently points out, 'the Islamic world has been unceasingly inconsolable in its destitution' (Meddeb, 2003) He argues that Islam knew one very high point of civilisation, accompanied by the boldness of hegemony, but that entropy has been at work since the fourteenth century. For him, Napoleon's successful expedition to Egypt brought home to many Muslims that they were not on a par with the western world. He traces a line of action and reaction through the decline of the Ottoman Empire, to the rise of Khomeini in Iran, and the Soviet invasion of Afghanistan to the present. These theories are not merely academic. In his pronouncements, Bin Laden makes frequent references to history and lambasts America and Britain as modern day crusaders who are intent on destroying Islam. The Gulf War and the invasions of Afghanistan and Iraq have further fuelled Muslim perception that the West's leaders are – however hard they may argue to the contrary – anti-Islamic.

Many non-Muslims, whilst not necessarily perceiving the coalition as anti-Muslim, still have great reservations about the actions undertaken. In his *Winning Modern Wars: Iraq, Terrorism and the American Empire*, Wesley K Clark, a US four star general and Vietnam veteran, provides an insight as to why some people might have great misgivings about the neocon world view of the most powerful nation on earth. Reviewing the book in the *Observer*, Jason Burke noted that Clark's believed that the Bush administration's bullish unilateralism, dependence on military force, disdain for international law and institutions have been profoundly counterproductive and run against everything that made America great. Clark argued that military power should be used only in the last resort and could only succeed in combination with diplomatic, social, political, economic, cultural and developmental measures. For him, '*the war on terror*' had only exacerbated the tensions, not ameliorated them' (November 2003, http://book.guardian.co.uk). The continued, seemingly endless, bloody aftermath of the invasion and occupation of Iraq have added further fuel to this argument.

In addition, the running sore of Palestine and of Lebanon, of terror and counter terror, of what appears to be unequivocal American support for Israel, further contribute to a perception that the west is profoundly anti-Islamic. Overlay these world events with the fifty year old argument between India and Pakistan over Kashmir, the religiously inspired atrocities in the Indian state of Gujarat, the arrival of significant numbers of Muslim asylum seekers from eastern Europe and Somalia and you have a potentially extremely explosive British cocktail. These contentious issues are the subject of *khutbah* (sermons) in many of our mosques and are very real to many British Muslim pupils and students.

Our Muslim pupils can also be subject to interpretations of the Qur'an and the traditions that justify extremist action. There are many pamphlets, books and websites which take sections of the Qur'an out of context and make universal truths of statements that, once analysed, are very much bound in time. Many of these are frighteningly anti-western and anti-Jewish in tone. For those who are disaffected and alienated from the society in which they find themselves, extremist calls to action and spurious promises of paradise can seem very attractive. Ed Husain in *The Islamist* (Husain, 2007) offers his own personal account of his journey in and out of radical Islam. He begins by quoting Muhammad (PBUH), 'Beware of extremism in religion; for it was extremism that destroyed those who went before you;' and goes on to explain what, as a British born adolescent, attracted him to radical Islam. For some time he saw himself as a Muslim living in Britain, rather than a British Muslim and was convinced of the imminent arrival of a new world order based on Islamic principles, a new caliphate where the *khaffar* (the unbeliever) would be overthrown. Husain outlines his gradual disaffection with this view, his move away from a conviction that was based upon intellect and political ideology towards one based upon the heart and love. In particular he cites the scholarship and classical arguments of Shaykh Hamza Yusuf Hanson of the Zaytuna Institute (www.zaytuna.org) and, partly because of his influence, returns to what he sees as the essence of Islam, 'spiritual surrender to serenity.'

Hassan Butt mirrors much of Husain's journey (July 2007, www.guardian.co. uk). For Butt, the great worry was not British foreign policy but the belief in the creation of a revolutionary state that would bring Islamic justice into the world. In the view of the Islamists, or what Butt calls the BJN (British Jihadi Network), in order to create such a state everything is permissible and justifiable in Qur'anic terms. Mohammed Sidique Khan, the quiet classroom assistant who was leader of the 7/7 bombers, expressed the view succinctly in a videotaped message released after the atrocities. 'We are at war and I am a soldier,' declared Khan. His motives were explicit. 'Your democratically elected governments continuously perpetuate atrocities against my people all over the world. And your support of them makes you directly responsible, just as I am directly responsible for protecting and avenging my Muslim brothers and sisters.' For Khan, his words were dead until he gave them life with his blood (http://news.bbc.co.uk).

It can be very difficult, however, for the ordinary British Muslim to understand some of the more esoteric arguments that surround what Khaled Abou el Fadl has called '*The Great Theft*', the hijacking of majority mainstream Muslim thought, practice and tradition ('the moderates') by a significant minority of what he calls Puritans (el Fadl, 2007). For Fadl, the consequences of the Puritan ideology have led directly to the 'ugly' manifestations of hijacking, terrorism and suicide bombings. Fadl's accessible and closely argued book explains, in lay terms, this battleground for faith, and charts the moderate versus the puritan divide. He argues that it has become imperative for Muslims to take a self-critical and introspective look at their own traditions, customs and beliefs in order to discover if 'the traditions of Islam ... contribute to the commission of these acts of ugliness'. For the American Fadl, and for many learned Muslims in the UK, 'the problem is that many Muslims are woefully ignorant about their own religion'. Traditionally *khutbah* in mosques do not encourage discussion, and young Muslims can be discouraged from discussing the sensitive issues like terrorism at home or in the mosques or madrasahs. As a number of young British Muslims reported at the Leicester Conference in September 2005, we are 'afraid to mention the 'T' word' and are 'scared to talk about terrorism' because of the way Muslims are already stereotyped. They were concerned that even a rational, objective discussion might leave them open to being labelled 'terrorist,' now a common term of abuse hurled at Muslims in British schools.

Much of the debate centres upon interpretations of the word jihad. In his presentation to the Jihad Conference in September 2003, Professor Richard Bonney echoes many Islamic scholars who, like Professor Fareed, urge

Muslims to 'develop the ability and the courage to look at Islamic documents with sharper eyes and in accordance with the needs of our time' (Bonney, 2004). For many scholars, the essential jihad is internal, the struggle of the soul against its own negative forces. There are real issues as to whom and in what circumstances a military jihad (often mistranslated as holy war) can be called and by whom. Mainstream Islamic scholars have vigorously challenged the whole legitimacy of extremist groups and individuals like Bin Laden.

In *The Quest for Sanity, Reflections on September 11th and the Aftermath*, the Muslim Council of Britain is unequivocally condemnatory of the events of 9/11, which it describes as 'simply evil and criminal' (MCB, 2002). As so many Muslims authors have done, it provides the Qur'anic references to demonstrate that Islam is fundamentally a religion of peace, tolerance, love, and justice. At the same time, Muslim scholars recognise that the essential Islamic values can, and must in certain defined circumstances, be forcibly defended. The series of articles from a range of Muslim and non-Muslim authors also provide insights into some of the global and other causes that can make fundamentalism attractive to some. The book chronicles the anti-Muslim racism perpetrated by sectors of the press and by individuals, and warns that the answer to such massive injustice is not more injustice, but actions based upon the international rule of law.

The rise and rise of Islamophobia

The events of 9/11 and of 7/7, the aftermath of the invasions of Afghanistan and Iraq, and the terrorist attacks throughout the world have led to an increase in anti-Muslim sentiment, expression and action. For many Muslims the wearing of *hijab*, or having beards or turbans, or any dress code that can vaguely be associated with Islam, has led to overt hostility. The comments about the veil as 'a visible statement of separation and difference' made by Jack Straw, a senior British government minister in the *Lancashire Evening Telegraph*, added fuel to this fire. In May 2002, the European Monitoring Centre on Racism and Xenophobia (EUMC) published a *Summary Report on Islamophobia in the EU after September 11th 2001*. The report

> unequivocally highlighted the regularity with which ordinary Muslims throughout Europe became indiscriminate targets for abusive and some times violent retaliatory attacks against them. A new ferocity and dynamism was clearly identified in the way in which Islamophobia became much more extreme, explicit and accepted across European society

Islamophobia is a relatively new term but a very old prejudice. It has little to do with Islam itself but is more about people's prejudiced perceptions of Islam. It was originally coined in the 1980s on an analogy with the word xeno-phobia (hostility towards foreigners). Historically anti-Muslim feeling has been a feature of European culture since the Crusades. Over time it has been used to justify acts of expansion and aggression against a range of countries and empires. Originally, Muslims were perceived as the enemy without, sometimes the enemy at the gate. More recently, with over 10 million Muslim citizens of the European Union, they have become for some, 'the enemy within'.

The term Islamophobia became widely known in Britain after the publication of a report by the Runnymede Trust, *Islamophobia – a challenge for us all* (Richardson *et al*, 1997). This well argued and balanced report made a clear distinction between legitimate debate and disagreement about Muslim beliefs and customs, a debate in which many Muslims themselves parti-cipate, in what the authors called 'open views of Islam' and between what they see as unfounded prejudice and hostility, the 'closed views of Islam'. They argued that anti-Muslim racism shares many of the features that are common to all racisms and hence is subject to Local Authority and school policies to counter racism and, more recently, religious discrimination. The report offers a thorough examination of the distinctions they make between 'closed' and 'open' views of Islam and argue that an irrational fear of Islam is the recurring characteristic of closed views. In summary form, the views of Islam focus upon:

- whether Islam is seen as monolithic and static, or as diverse and dynamic

- whether Islam is seen as 'other' and separate, or as similar and inter-dependent

- whether Islam is seen as inferior, or as different but equal

- whether Islam is seen as an aggressive enemy, or as a co-operative partner

- whether Muslims are seen as manipulative, or as sincere

- whether Muslim criticisms of the west are rejected, or debated

- whether discriminatory behaviour against Muslims is defended or opposed

■ whether anti-Muslim comments, stereotypes and discourse are seen as natural and 'common sense', or as problematic and to be challenged

■ whether no account is taken of the fact that Muslims have limited access to the media

■ whether unequal freedom of expression is recognised

The report's Chapter 4: *Media coverage* in particular reveals very worrying trends in reporting on Islamic issues. The authors examined a vast number of references to Islam in the press and concluded that 'closed' views were routinely reflected in both broadsheets and tabloids, in the local and national press, and in the whole panoply of editorials, comment, letters and cartoons. Many Muslims found it very difficult to see themselves reflected at all, whether in TV soaps, or as reporters or commentators, or in journalism which effectively looked at the range of Islamic opinion. The follow-up report, *Islamophobia: Issues, Challenges and Action* (Uniting Britain Trust 2004), and a range of other articles by Richardson (www.insted.co.uk) provide further examples of its growing invidious and insidious nature, and offer a range of practical guidance to combat it. Similarly, the Muslim Council of Britain monitors the situation in the UK and also provides support to try to counter both the causes and the effects.

In spite of the efforts of people like Richardson and the MCB, Islamophobia is on the increase. It had become so serious by 2005 that a not for profit project, *Islamophobia Watch*, was founded to document material in the public domain which advocates fear and hatred of the Muslim peoples of the world and Islam as a religion. Accessing the site's many articles starkly reveals the contemporary level of the problem, almost a decade after the Runnymede Trust's first detailed analysis. The launch by Tim Brighouse of the MCB's seminal document, *Towards Greater Understanding: Meeting the needs of Muslim pupils in state schools* (MCB, 2007) elicited the most negative response possible from the *Daily Express*, who wrote that the MCB were advocating 'Taliban-style' conditions in state schools. Richardson's analysis (2007) of the *Express* article and its Islamophobic responses reveal the extent of the problem.

The history of racism appears to repeat itself in different guises. The arguments that were fought and won (at least by many schools and authorities) in the 1980s and 1990s to persuade schools and LEAs to tackle direct, indirect and institutional racism have now to be restated within an Islamic context.

Failure to tackle Islamophobia is another form of miseducation because of the alienation it causes. It wastes talent, causes hurt and grief to the victims and leaves the perpetrators with a false sense of their own superiority. A worldview that sees over 1.6 million of the UK's population as alien, different, 'the enemy within' is not sustainable in a multicultural, multi-faith inclusive society. Unless systematically tackled, it is likely to breed levels of resentment that lead to violent resistance, which in turn can lead to increased racism as the consequence of such violence. The cycle can and does all too easily repeat itself.

The race equality perspective

Birmingham City Council is typical of a number of LEAs who, over a long period of time, have attempted to address the needs of Muslim pupils within a wider multicultural perspective. As long ago as 1988 the Authority, in partnership with local representatives from the Muslim Liaison Committee (MLC), devised a comprehensive set of *Guidelines on Meeting the Religious and Cultural Needs of Muslims*, revised by the MLC in 1999 (Birmingham City Council 1999). These guidelines focused on Islamic cultural issues, such as modesty, the wearing of clothing with religious significance and dietary needs. They offered practical advice and a resolution reference point in potential cases of conflict and concentrated upon issues of collective worship, the provision of prayer facilities, festivals, *halal* meat and sex education. In balanced and measured terms they urged schools to bear in mind that Muslim parents may have strong reservations about the kind of relationships between boys and girls, particularly at the age of 10 and over, that are customary in our schools; and urged that schools

> be aware that certain curricular areas of experience, such as health education, drama and physical education (in particular, gymnastics, swimming and dance in mixed classes) and certain fund-raising activities, including lotteries and gambling, might need careful consideration and discussion with parents if confidence in the school is to be maintained.

In addition, they urge schools to adhere to the principle of modesty for both sexes, especially where common showers and changing facilities are concerned. The guidelines were clearly located within the framework of the LEA's multicultural antiracist policy and the Religious Education syllabi agreed by SACRE (the Standing Advisory Council for Religious Education). Birmingham, probably like most authorities at that time, did not extend the guidelines to cover the wider issues of underperformance or the complex and sensitive issues of British Muslim identities.

Leicester's Islam and Education Network, writing in 2007, however, addresses many of these more contentious issues head on. Their *Faith and Education: Responding to school based issues Islam* (Billingham, 2007) offer detailed content and process advice on areas of the curriculum, on dress, festivals and pilgrimages and on a range of sensitive issues like forced marriages and female genital mutilation. The advice is non prescriptive, sensitively presented and aims to support schools in a collaborative partnership with parents and the community. Leicester acknowledges their great debt to the Muslim Council of Britain's *Towards Greater understanding: Meeting the needs of Muslim pupils in state schools* (MCB, 2007).

This detailed and well argued guidance offers advice in all areas of school life and is predicated upon a Muslim inclusive approach. For the MCB, 'it is essential that positive account is taken of the faith dimension of Muslim pupils in education and schooling. The faith of Muslim pupils should be seen as an asset to addressing constructively many of the issues young people face today...' Both Leicester City Council and the MCB explain how meeting the needs of Muslim pupils helps schools fulfil their statutory duties.

Most authorities with large numbers of minority ethnic pupils have used various statutory clauses to reinforce the legitimacy of their own antiracist policies. It has been unlawful to discriminate directly or indirectly on the basis of race since the Race Relations Act of 1976. In law, racial includes race, colour, nationality (including citizenship), and ethnic or national origins. It took almost 25 years and the tragic racist murder of black teenager Stephen Lawrence to transform a negative 'you shall not', into a positive 'you must'. The Race Relations (Amendment) Act 2000 placed a statutory duty on public authorities and educational institutions to promote race equality. It prescribed a general duty on authorities to build race equality into the day-to-day work of public services, and prescribed certain specific duties on all those involved in delivering education services. Schools, for example, are now required to prepare a written statement of their policy for promoting race equality and to monitor and assess its impact on pupils, parents and staff of different racial groups, in particular the impact on attainment levels of such pupils.

These statutory demands are reinforced in the most recent Ofsted framework and handbooks for inspecting schools, as inspectors are required to assess how far statutory arrangements and policies are in place. In addition, section 3.1 requires inspectors to interpret and report on the standards achieved in the areas of learning, subjects and courses of the curriculum generally, and in particular to assess the relative achievement of different groups and individuals, especially those from different ethnic backgrounds and those whose home language is not English. Inspectors also judge pupils' personal development and comment on the extent to which pupils are free from bullying, racism and other forms of harassment which by inference must include religious harassment. They also assess 'the extent to which the school actively enables pupils to develop self knowledge and spiritual awareness ... and appreciate their own and others' cultural traditions.'

Although no explicit reference is made to religion, inspectors will comment on the range of ethnic groups who can obviously be identified as Muslim. For Ofsted, the key judgments concern whether the achievements of pupils are as high as they should be, taking into account their capabilities and the progress they have made. Achievements include pupils' knowledge, skills and understanding gained through the subjects of the curriculum often measured by national attainment tests; and the attitudes, behaviour and development fostered by the school.

The attainment perspective

Increasingly sophisticated collection of Key Stage 2 and GCSE attainment figures based upon ethnicity have demonstrated that there is a significant attainment gap between national and local averages and the performance of various groups. Although there is no national data cross-tabulating educational attainment with religious affiliation, the local and national pictures indicate that two under attaining groups Pakistani/Kashmiri origin and Bangladeshis origin are Muslim. These two groups make up two thirds of the 1.6 million 'Muslims in Britain' who were identified on census night 2001. There is relatively little statistical data available about the other third. Some are of Indian, largely Gujarati origin, the majority of whom reside in Leicester; others are from African countries, particularly Somalia and the remainder is principally from Turkey, North Africa and the Middle East. There is a small but growing number of white and African-Caribbean converts.

The extension of the DfES *Aiming High* strategy to Pakistani, Bangladeshis, Somali and Turkish pupils in 2004 became known as MEAP, the Minority Ethnic Achievement Project. One factor common to these groups was their faith background. The other was their comparative levels of underachievement. MEAP marked a positive response to the fact that these groups generally achieve poorer GCSE results than other groups, with the exception of the African-Caribbean population, that these gaps are apparent at the end of Key Stage 2, and that for these groups the gaps widen further during secondary education. The overall figures mask the reality that the under-performance of pupils of Pakistani/Kashmiri heritage 'predominantly situated in the Midlands and the Northern towns' are significantly greater than the national figures suggest. This, and the responses of fifteen local authorities to the challenge, was highlighted in the RAISE report, *The Achievement of British Pakistani Learners* (Richardson and Wood, 2004).

The MEAP project began as a pilot in October 2004, built upon the RAISE insights. It involved twelve local authorities and 52 schools nationally and targeted Key Stage 3 pupils. Its success led to the involvement of more authorities and schools. Progress in raising attainment has been significant and a series of newsletters chart these developments. A management guide was issued in March 2007 which offered intervention strategies that could be replicated elsewhere (*Raising the attainment of Pakistani, Bangladeshi, Somali; and Turkish heritage pupils, a management guide* DfES, 2007).

Local Authorities are required to address attainment gaps as part of their Children and Young People's Plans and they, like schools, are assessed by Ofsted on the success of the various strategies and initiatives they have put into place to raise the achievement of their under performing groups. They will also be assessed on how their schools are promoting community cohesion which became a statutory duty for schools in September 2007.

The Community Cohesion perspective

Community Cohesion as a term is not new, but its contemporary relevance was highlighted after the disturbances in 2001 which began at Easter in Bradford but by early summer had spread to Oldham, Leeds, Burnley, Bradford (again) and Stoke on Trent. There were obvious racial overtones to the disturbances, as those involved were predominantly white and Asian youths. That the majority of the Asian young people involved were of Pakistani/ Kashmiri heritage adds a Muslim dimension. In response, the Home Office commissioned a report to try to discover the underlying causes and recommend possible solutions. A team led by Ted Cantle (*Community Cohesion: A report of the independent review team*, 2002) made extensive visits not only to the riot-torn areas but also to cities like Leicester and Birmingham which have addressed some of these issues more successfully. Their findings, like those of Swann fifteen years earlier, not only reflect much of what the minority ethnic communities have been articulating for a long time but also gave voice to those disadvantaged white communities who feel disenfranchised and disempowered. Cantle's overriding and somewhat frightening conclusion was that, in spite of all the funding and good intentions, the outcome was often the very opposite of the intention. In summary, Cantle found that:

- separate educational arrangements, community and voluntary bodies, employment, places of worship, language, social and cultural networks, mean that many communities operate on the basis of a series of parallel lives

- the plethora of initiatives and programmes, with their baffling array of outcomes, boundaries, timescales and other conditions seemed to ensure divisiveness and a perception of unfairness in virtually every section of the communities we visited

- many community-based schemes – including those developed and run by statutory agencies – seemed to be clinging on to the margins of anything that resembled a longer term strategy

- area based regeneration in some cases reinforced the separation of communities

- opportunities were far from equal in respect of housing, employment and education

To counter this fragmentation, Cantle proposed a wide-ranging strategy which included a well-resourced national debate, heavily influenced by younger people, based upon a new concept of citizenship, with a coherent approach to education, housing, regeneration, employment and other programmes. These would be delivered locally via a local community cohesion plan that would promote cross cultural contact and strong local leadership. Cantle was clear that extensive diversity education in all key agencies would be required. In all, Cantle and his team recommended 67 practical measures to be put in place by a range of agencies. Most precisely, Cantle argued that, 'the emphasis should switch over time to school-based schemes (and outreach from schools) to prevent disaffection and underachievement at the earliest possible stage' (Home Office, 2002). Cantle summed up this strategic approach as promoting 'community cohesion'.

Community cohesion incorporates and goes beyond the concept of social cohesion. It is closely linked to other concepts like inclusion and exclusion, social capital and differentiation, community and neighbourhood. Race equality is implicit in many of its central themes, especially those that relate to diversity and interfaith dialogue. The Local Government Association, in its comprehensive and helpful document, *Guidance on Community Cohesion* (2002) offers a broad and useful definition of a cohesive community. Their broad working definition of a cohesive community is one where:

- there is a common vision and sense of belonging for all communities

- the diversity of people's different backgrounds and circumstances are appreciated and positively valued

- those from different backgrounds have similar opportunities

- Strong and positive relationships are being developed from different backgrounds in the workplace, in schools and within neighbourhoods

The Commission on Integration and Cohesion, in their comprehensive *Our Shared Futures* report to central government (www.integrationandcohesion. org) breaks down this original definition into more detail, identifying a cohesive community as one where 'there is a clearly defined and widely shared sense of the contribution of different individuals and different communities to a future vision for a neighbourhood, city, region or country.' The commission felt it important to recognise the contribution made by individuals, whilst acknowledging that they will hold different ambitions, aspirations, beliefs and experiences. It also placed strong emphasis on how they will share important characteristics and experiences with those from their own and other communities. The Commission's report also underlines the importance of rights and responsibilities, and of equality, in terms of both addressing the equality gaps and ensuring fair and transparent treatment for all communities. The DCSF in their non-statutory *Guidance on the Duty to Promote Community Cohesion* (DCSF, 2007) are clear about the importance of school in helping to achieve these aims: 'Schools' role here is crucial: by creating opportunities for pupils' achievement and enabling every child and young person to achieve their potential, schools make a significant contribution to long term community cohesion.'

For the Department, 'community' includes all the stakeholders involved in the school community itself; the wider community in which the school is based; and the UK and global communities. Their guidance groups the schools' contribution under three broad headings of teaching, learning and the curriculum; equity and excellence; and engagement and extended services. Engagement and extended services' is particularly pertinent to Muslims, especially those in the northern cities, as it encourages schools 'to provide reasonable means for children, their families and friends to interact with people from different backgrounds and build positive relations: including links with different schools and communities'.

Some Local Authorities like Oldham and Bradford have already developed well orchestrated and structures twining programmes to ensure that for their children and young people, 'parallel lives' will no longer be the reality. The Bradford schools Linking Project provides an excellent model (www.bradford schools.net).

Although the Cantle report and the debate and funding that followed it have been welcomed, not all commentators applauded the report. Farzana Shain (2003) is highly critical of the political context. She asserts that 'racism is caused by segregation rather than causing it. The picture that emerges is of racism as being caused by the failure of particular groups to integrate' (Shain, 2003). Here is another racist example of 'blaming the victim'. She locates her trenchant criticisms within the demonising of Muslim communities across the globe and is particularly critical of Home Secretary David Blunkett's pronouncements on religion, integration and 'moral relativism'. For her, what emerges from 'Blunkett's proclamations is an image of an isolated (mainly Muslim) community that clings to backward practices, does not bother to learn the English language and does not want to integrate into mainstream society'. The old image of the hardworking passive Asian (Muslim) boy has been transformed over time to one of an aggressive, volatile, hot headed fundamentalist.

The Muslim perspectives

Shain's chapter on 'New Racisms, Old Pathologies' charts the radicalisation of black and Asian youth over time. Drawing on the work of Saghal and Yuval-Davis (1992), she argues that the Rushdie affair has played a crucial role in the politicisation of Muslim identity. Groups that had previously identified themselves by ethnic origin (Pakistani, Mirpuri, and Punjabi) have since been defined primarily by religion, that is, as Muslims. Other writers have sought to explain the intensity of the different levels of Muslim reaction to *The Satanic Verses* across the country, particularly concentrating on the racial, working class and deprived position of Bradford youth, the area which saw the most vehement response to the book. Without doubt, many Muslims, even those who were not practising, were offended by sections of a book that appeared to cast doubt over the authenticity of the Qur'an and to impugn the virtues of the wives of the Messenger (PBUH). Bradford's reaction was the most extreme. It was argued that this was because levels of unemployment were so high amongst youths of Mirpuri origin and because the Muslim community was already smarting over the negative remarks made about them by Ray Honeyford, one of the city's headteachers.

The Honeyford and Rushdie affairs perhaps marked a watershed in the politicisation of Muslim identity, certainly within the UK. Since then, world events have increasingly led Muslim youth, both girls and boys, to reassess their position and increasingly choose to see themselves as Muslim first. The conscious decision by many young women to wear *hijab* and by many young men to adopt Muslim dress styles is one overt manifestation of this trend.

The problem for Muslim youth is that Islam is not a homogenous one size fits all religion. Its sectarian and doctrinal divisions are potentially deep and complicated. Fundamentalist, anti- western statements can seem attractive to British Muslim youth, especially those who feel disaffected and disempowered. Britain's Muslims, like Europe's, are a 'community of communities' (Parekh, 2002). They can divide by ethnic, cultural, linguistic and historical factors that often mean that outside their faith background they have little in common. Even within the faith, there can be huge difference between *Sunni* and *Shi'ah*, between *Barelvis* and *Deobandis*, between the *Wahhabis* and the *Sufis*. Mohammad S. Raza (1991) argues that sectarianism seems to have become serious in Britain. It has become so, he believes, because many Muslims are reacting to a predominantly secular society in which they fear they will lose their children to western values. Their response is to cling to sectarian affiliations that in turn have increased rivalries, which clearly defeats one aspect of being Muslim, that is being a part of united community known as the *ummah*.

The Ummah

The great irony is that the Muslim community, although divided in many ways, does see itself as a community, as the *ummah*. It is perhaps difficult for a non-Muslim to appreciate the degree of commonality and the common bonds that exist for the *ummah*. Jonathan Raban, writing in the *Guardian* April 19 2003, eloquently and passionately describes the working of the *ummah* in the context of Iraq where he attempts to explain why the international body of believers has been so vitalised by its own pain and rage. As he explains, the idea of the body is central here:

> It would be a great mistake to read this as mere metaphor or rhetorical flourish. *Ummah* is sometimes defined as the community, sometimes the nation, sometimes the body of Muslim believers around the globe, and it has a physical reality, without parallel in any other religion, that is nowhere better expressed than in the five daily times of prayer.

There are many rituals and daily practices that unite the five billion Muslims worldwide. They are all called to prayer in a similar way. They all use Arabic for the five daily prayers, for the Qur'anic readings, for the sayings attributed to the Prophet (PBUH). They all undergo the ritual ablution (*wudu*) in a similar way. They pray in a similar way, facing the *Qibla* in *Makkah* and prostrating themselves at given moments of prayer according to a precise formula. They have common expectations of giving to the poor, of fasting during Ramadan, of performing *Hajj* (pilgrimage) at least once in their lives, where regardless of class, colour, wealth they all dress alike and perform the given rituals alike. Internet web sites like the Islamic finder provide prayer times for five million cities worldwide and for major cities and towns in the UK. Arabic terms like '*insha'allah*' (God willing) and '*masha'allah*' (by the will of Allah) punctuate the speech patterns of many Muslims whatever home language they speak. Qur'anic values determine much of what is said and done. It would be difficult to overestimate the impact of Islam in the daily pattern of many Muslim's lives. The daily prayers, even when said at home, can take up to an hour a day to perform.

The Belief that Unites

That is not to say that all Muslims are devout and that all Muslims think alike. Given the insecurities and divisions that exist within the Islamic world, the UK, Europe and elsewhere that would be nonsense. Islam is, however, a broad mosque. It is probably true to say that there is more that unites Muslims than divides them. Regardless of doctrinal differences, all Muslims share the core belief that 'There is none worthy of worship but God, and Muhammad is God's Messenger' (the *Shahadah*). This faith is the first and most important element of Muslim identity. Closely linked to faith is the fundamental dimension of spirituality, which is the way in which the believer keeps alive, intensifies and strengthens faith. In Islamic terms, spirituality is about remembering God, about reciting His names and observing the prayers and other rituals as a way to remember (the *dhikr*). Crucially, it has also developed a socio-political dimension in terms of establishing and maintaining justice and piety in social institutions.

Faith has to be lived to be real. The Prophet (PBUH) lived his faith and taught his faith daily. He constantly demonstrated that love, bounty, generosity and justice were the true values and repeated to his Companions that they should be good to one another, respect all living beings, nature and, most importantly of all, treat with equity all Muslims or non-Muslims, men or women, young or old. The Prophet stressed the importance of family values, of kindness and of tolerance, 'No one among you attains true Faith, until he likes for his brother what he likes for himself' and, 'He is not a true Believer who eats his fill while his neighbour is hungry'.

There are examples of the prophet administering justice in favour of Jews and other non-Muslims over Muslims, as the faithful have to be strict defenders of justice regardless of faith background. 'Behold God enjoins justice, and excellence (sincerity)'. In Islam, this goes beyond the simple implementation of overt justice and moves into remembrance and the link with God, so as to nourish the notion of justice and bring the Believer closer to the love and compassion of God. This is the central message in Tariq Ramadan's *The Messenger: The Meaning of the life of Muhammad* (2007) where he aims to make the Prophet's life a mirror through which readers facing contemporary challenges can explore their hearts and minds and achieve an understanding of questions of being and meaning, as well as broader ethical and social concerns. Like el Fadl, Ramadan challenges Muslims to move from formalism – a fixation on the rituals of Islam – to a deeper understanding of its spiritual and social presence. For him,

> the prophet's life is an invitation to a spirituality that avoids no question and teaches us ... that the true answers to existential questions are more often given by the heart than by intelligence. Deeply, simply: he who cannot love cannot understand

There is a real need for teachers and for local and central government officers to understand the *Muslim Frame of Reference* and use it to help their pupils understand and deal with the issues that preoccupy many British Muslims. That frame of reference has two major foundations: the Qur'an, the divine revelation that was given to the Prophet Muhammad (PBUH) over a 23-year period; and the *Sunnah*. The *Sunnah* is the traditions and practices of Muhammad (PBUH) and the first generation of Muslims, which include the *hadith* – the collections of the Messenger's reported sayings. In addition, generations of scholars, known as *ulama*, have sought to interpret texts and to agree upon interpretations through *ijma* (consensus) and *qiyas* (analogy). These four sources provide the canonical basis for Muslim belief and practice.

'For many Muslims in the UK, Islam is the key determinant in their lives' (DfES, 2006). Yet schools are not always sensitive to this. As they enter through the school portals, pupils are required to leave their religion at home, not through design but because so often the school, as a secular institution, is unaware of the centrality of Islam in the life of its Muslim pupils. There is a great and understandable reluctance to begin to debate what it means to be a British Muslim. Some Muslims would disagree with the concept altogether and argue that they are Muslims in Britain, presumably looking to a better place to practise their religion, 'whose hearts and minds are overseas' (Seddon, Hussain and Malik, 2003). Similarly, many teachers do not feel equipped to help steer their pupils through the complicated Islamic mine-field, both groups perhaps fearful that they might open an Islamic Pandora's box and unleash forces they would be unable to control. But such are the forces, pressures and influences on young Muslims that schools must grasp the nettle and engage in open and honest dialogue about what it means to be a British Muslim. The discourse must be one between equals, not one that assumes one set of values is superior to another.

The pressures and influences on young Muslims

In many ways there has never been a more difficult time to be a young Muslim growing up in the UK. Identity is fashioned by a range of often-conflicting demands depending on the context of the family, the ethnic group, the school, the peer group, and the faith. The country of their parents' origin is often another variable. Increasingly, we live in a world of multiple identities so that, depending on the context if which we find ourselves, the Kashmiri Pakistani, or the Mirpuri or the Brummie aspects of our identity are prevalent. For Muslims however, Faith is the key determinant. How and what children learn is mediated by the family and their understanding – or lack of it – of Islam, and the mosque and the mosque schools with which they are associated.

At least up to the age of 14, most children will attend one of these schools. The issues for most young Muslims is that the pedagogical style is very different from that with which they are familiar in maintained schools, as it places the greatest emphasis on learning and reciting the Qur'an in Arabic by heart and there is generally little discussion as to meaning and interpretation. Many imams and teachers in the mosque received their education outside the UK and many Muslim communities send for and pay compatriots from their homeland to undertake these teaching tasks. There is an increasing percep-tion that many of these teachers are simply not equipped to advise their charges on issues such as growing up in the UK, the education of girls, drugs, or unemployment and youth culture. Adolescence is difficult for all those passing through it. It is even more difficult if you do not share a common lan-guage and common experiences with those to whom you may look for guidance.

Muslims may turn to local and national youth organisations, which seek to promote the Muslim faith within the setting of a non-Muslim country such as Britain. Many have their own web sites and use English as the main medium of discourse. For many, there is a disparity between what they hear and learn from such organisations and what they were told at the mosque or by their families. Some are attracted to extremist organisations and fundamentalist interpretations of Islam, both of which can be simplistically anti-western and crudely anti-Jewish. There is limited knowledge as to how many extremist groups there are, largely because many of them are underground in nature, and the suspicion is that the media overstates their importance. It is important to know; however, that these views have currency and can seem very attractive to those seeking what they consider is a more Islamic identity within a framework of resistance.

Young Muslims, like any other group, can be and are being drawn into their own street culture that seems attractive, especially to those who are unemployed and have few qualifications, so have little obvious means of escaping economic deprivation. The largely secular mainstream culture and the Islamophobic messages that Muslims receive can undermine, or reinforce, the young people's sense of identity sense as Muslims. As one Muslim periodical put it,

> For many youngsters Islam is proving to be a genuine way out, a way to make sense of the bewildering maelstrom of currents surrounding them. For many others, it is a reactionary garb as something they see as a source of opposition. The irony is that by demonising Muslims the mass media is also erecting a romantic notion of opposition to mainstream culture (cited in the *Runnymede Trust Bulletin*, 1997).

Chapter 2 of the *RAISE project*, outlines the contemporary influences and potential conflicts and choices that young British Muslims face as they grow up in 21st century Britain. (RAISE 2004). Strong echoes of these views are to be found in *Faithful and Proud, the Young British Muslim conference report* (Coles, 2005). This provided one of the clearest statements yet of how young British Muslims perceive themselves and the world in which they live.

Islam and democracy

Debates about the nature of Islam and its place in the West are not confined to youths. They are reflected at a geo-political level and resonate in comments and actions made by President Bush and former Prime Minister Blair, who continually stress that their war is a 'war on terror', and not a war on a great religion. For some, recent terrorist events have born out their interpretation of Samuel Huntington's thesis (2002) which identified Islam as one of the threats to western hegemony. This interpretation of Islam however, was strongly challenged at the time by many Islamic scholars. The seeming clash of cultures between Muslim values and Western values has been the subject of fierce debate, a debate that goes to the very heart of Muslims and democracy.

Tariq Ramadan, in his comprehensive work, *To be a European Muslim – A Study of Islamic Sources in the European Context* (1994), seeks to answer some of the basic questions about European Muslims' social, political, cultural and legal integration. With his thorough knowledge of Islamic sources, he demonstrates that it is possible to lead life as a practising Muslim while living together in multi-faith, pluralistic European nation states. The situation in which Muslims find themselves in Europe, a direct legacy of European economic and geographic imperialism, has obliged many to think closely about the implications of their faith and its daily practice. This in turn has led to the reopening of questions that had faced Muslim scholars and thinkers at the height of Muslim civilisation a thousand years ago, and has always troubled Muslims living outside Muslim countries. Ironically, those living on the margins of the Muslim world have perforce returned to the theological centre to seek answers. Increasingly Muslim youths are asking fundamental questions about the place of Islam in England and in the world and seek to know more about Muslim civilisation and its legacy.

First generation immigrants, in a strange and hostile environment and often with a very limited knowledge of Islam, tried to conserve what they saw as essential Islamic values in what appeared to be a permissive, even promiscuous, land. Many clung to *cultural Islam*, that is, to the particular practices, customs and faith interpretations which had more to do with their country of origin than with essential doctrine. As Ramadan argues, one finds the scars of this attitude among younger generations and these can manifest themselves in 'self assertion, very often linked with a total oblivion of one's origins and attempts to remain faithful to Islamic references as translated both in thinking and in action, by reaction, rejection, refusal and sometimes aggression' (Ramadan 1994). For some youths the measure of their faith is proportionate to their rejection of the west, as if they defined Islam by what it is not, rather than what it is. They can reduce their religion to a series of prescriptions and rules, to listing what is permitted and lawful (*halal*) and unlawful (*haram*). Their own search for Islamic truth is often hampered by their limited knowledge of Arabic and by a lack of understanding of the Qur'an and the ahadith that they are encouraged to recite but generally not encouraged to interpret.

Ramadan maintains that many Muslims have internalised the negative perceptions of themselves as 'the problem': 'It is as if ... they have been colonised by the idea, the obvious fact, the indisputable evidence that Islam is a problem in the West and that Muslims have problems with progress, democracy and modernity.' On the positive side, there is an increasing tendency for young Muslims to assert their faith identity but this is counterbalanced by a feeling that they are unable to contribute to the Western Muslim debate and seek their answers from interpretations of the Qur'an, a*hadith* and the subsequent exegetical canons of Islamic law and jurisprudence (the *Fiqh*) that over time have been made by generations of learned Muslim scholars, known collectively as the *ulama*. 'We are witnessing, among young European Muslims, the unhealthy development of a complex whereby they discredit themselves and think that the right responses should come from abroad, from great '*ulama*' residing in Islamic countries.'

Ramadan's technical though highly readable book outlines in some detail the essential values and teachings of Islam and Islamic Sciences. His essential argument is that it is within the tradition for Muslims to discuss how to adapt and adopt their faith to different circumstances, to the vicissitudes of changing times, provided of course the essentials of the faith are retained. In Islam there is great respect for tradition and for scholarly knowledge. The absolute nature of the core principles is not open to debate, but this is balanced against the need to interpret those principles in the local contemporary context. Indeed it is God's will that religious diversity exists and to each people he gave a specific message:

> Unto every one of you have We appointed a different law way of life. And if God had so willed, He could have surely have made you all one single community: but (He willed it otherwise) in order to test you by means of what he vouchsafed unto you. Vie, then with one another in doing good works. (Qur'an 5:48)

Soon after his flight from *Makkah* to *Madinah* the Prophet, after consultation with various groups in the region, drew up a document called the *Sahifah*, which has been described as the first written constitution in the world. This constitution legalised a pluralist, multiracial, multicultural society comprising Jews and Muslims. All sectors of the community had the freedom to practise their religion, to earn a living as they saw fit and were bound by a series of obligations and responsibilities. It was a physical embodiment of Islamic ideals of justice and democracy and laid the foundations of the tolerance that characterised much of the period of Muslim hegemony.

On the face of it, much of this discourse may appear to be esoteric but issues of citizenship and how we promote it go to the very heart of how we as a nation see ourselves, of how we as educators promote citizenship, and how Muslims perceive education.

The Muslim view of learning and knowledge

'Education should ... cater for the growth of 'man' in all its aspects: Spiritual, intellectual, imaginative, physical, scientific, linguistic, both individually and collectively and motivate. All these aspects contribute towards goodness and the attainment of perfection' (Haw, 1998). Unsurprisingly, such a view is in accord with how non-Muslims see education, especially as 'man' in the Qur'an has been interpreted as non-gendered, referring to both men and women when used collectively. It is probably true, however, that most non-Muslims are unlikely to write about the drive to goodness and the attainment of perfection, even though this may be implicit in the values of our education system. That emphasis is the essential difference: not that Muslim education negates or denies that which we see as traditionally Western but rather that its overarching goal is attuned to faith in action which in its turn continually leads Muslims to remember God. For Muslims, the ultimate goal is to seek God through Knowledge (*ilm*). Haw, (1998) neatly encapsulates the Islamic difference between 'revealed knowledge' and 'acquired knowledge.' Revealed knowledge is part of the absolute knowledge that is of God and is granted to only a few. For Muslims, the last revelation was to Muhammad (PBUH) himself when Archangel Gabriel delivered the Qur'an to him over a 23-year period. Much of Islamic scholarship is dedicated to interpretations of this revelation. Acquired knowledge on the other hand relates to social, natural and applied sciences but must be firmly placed within the context of revelation.

What is undisputed is that the entire *hadith* literature is replete with references from the Qur'an and the sayings of the Prophet which urge believers of both genders to gain knowledge: 'Seeking knowledge is compulsory for every Muslim, man and woman' (*hadith*). 'Seek knowledge even unto China' (*hadith*). The Prophet's favourite supplication was reported to have been: 'O my Lord, increase me in my knowledge'. Al-Bukhari attributes a tradition to the prophet which says that the disappearance of knowledge and the absence of scholars from society would spell the demise of civilisation.

Traditionally, Islam has insisted that reason and revelations are the two drivers in life's quest and in order to reach one's destination both have to be pursued. The search for knowledge can be seen as an act of piety, as equivalent to prayer. The ultimate use of the intellect is the cultivation of the divine attributes and the role of knowledge in the religio-political life of the *ummah* is decisive and all pervading. It ennobles, enriches and solidifies faith and belief in the revealed word of Allah. Theoretically, all Muslims are under a religious obligation to accept learning as a continuous process in life, and early

Muslims were encouraged to use independent judgement based on the righteous intention to overcome the difficulties of life.

It was due to the insistence on research and enquiry as a religious duty that early Muslims produced some of the greatest early scientific works and developed a great civilisation. Without this scientific knowledge, many of the religious duties and ceremonies would not have been possible, as so much of it is based on intricate calculations of the lunar calendar and many of the complex laws of Islam required considerable knowledge of diverse sciences. Without careful scholarship, much of it comparative, Muslim scholars could not fulfil their duty to God.

Education, women and Islam

Perhaps there is nothing that arouses so much passion amongst non-Muslims as the perceived position of women in Islam and their treatment by men. For many, the taking of the veil, the wearing of the *hijab*, the demands for single sex schooling are all symbols of a male-dominated culture that circumscribes female freedom and which, in some Gulf States and in Taliban Afghanistan, represent the very antithesis of western democratic freedoms. It is important to make a distinction between cultural Islam – that is the traditions, practices, habits that have grown up over time in particular cultural contexts and which probably have limited justification in the Qur'an or a*hadith* – and Islam that is more closely based upon Qur'anic teachings. Many of the practices that some find offensive appear to owe more to culture than to religion. Saeeda Shah (1998) details some of the responsibilities and the limits. Thus, the Qur'an does not command sex segregation but does describe appropriate dress and behaviour codes, specifically for mixed contexts. Seeking knowledge is *fard* (obligatory) for both sexes, and there is evidence that the Prophet (PBUH) and his wife A'ishah taught mixed sex groups.

The importance of Islamic civilisation and its place in the mainstream curriculum

It is probably a truism that for their own sense of self-esteem and worth all pupils need to see themselves reflected positively in the curriculum of the schools they attend. Muslims will find this in the 125 or so independent Muslim schools, an increasing number of which are applying for and receiving voluntary-aided status. It is definitely far from the case in mainstream schools generally. Many pupils could go through most, if not all, their educational career without coming into contact with the wealth and legacies of the great age of Islamic civilisation. Islamic civilisation flourished from Spain to

Central Asia in its first thousand years. While Europe suffered what has been called the Dark Ages, Muslims translated, enhanced and developed much of the thinking of the ancient Greeks and made remarkable contributions in the realms of science, medicine, art and architecture, literature and astrology. Many of the greatest Sufi mystical tracts and poetry were also written during this period, in particular, the works of the great Persian Sufi poet, Rumi. Rumi's poetry, such as his *Mathnawi*, has great contemporary appeal and is reported to be the fastest selling work in the USA.

Many of these great achievements are succinctly documented in Bloom and Blair's book, written to accompany a BBC 2 series on Islam in 2001. But they make no attempt to assess Islam's contribution to the modern world. Increasingly, Islamic scholars are taking up this challenge and are cogently arguing that the roots of modern world with its emphasis on liberty and freedoms, science and technology, owe much to Muslim scholarship and research. Professor Salim T S Al Hassani, of the Foundation for Technology and Science takes up what is now becoming a key theme: *One Thousand Years of Missing History* (www.muslimheritage.com). He argues that European historians have generally ignored the link between the ancient Greeks, Islamic civilisation and the European renaissance and enlightenment. Yet Europe owes a great debt to the Muslim scholars who translated key texts from the Greek, developed medicine, founded the first universities and were responsible for a great flowering of intellectual thought. This contribution has been wonderfully well documented in an exhibition and book which accompanies it, *1001 Inventions: Muslim Heritage in our World* (FTSC, 2006). In seven chapters it chronicles the crucial Muslim contribution to our contemporary world in the areas of home, school, market, hospital, town, world and the universe. This foundation is working with a number of local authorities, subject associations and the QCA to produce a range of resources for schools (www.1001 inventions.com) in a project which has become known as CUSP.

The major question western Muslims ask – and will ask even more insistently when the school system effectively acknowledges the debt we all owe to Muslim scholarship – and that perplexes many writers and scholars is: what happened? What happened to Islam that led to its decline, to its rude shocks when the military vanguard of another and alien culture, defeated it so comprehensively over such a long period of time? The answer is as complex as the question is simple. Huge tomes and learned treatises relate the decline of Islamic civilisation to a diverse range of economic, industrial, military and other causes.

For educationalists, however, one of the key factors appears to have been the alleged ending of *ijtihad*, normally translated as independent reasoning or thinking. As Shaukat Ali (1993) says 'the closing of the doors of *ijtihad* was the single most important factor which killed the spirit of enquiry'. Others, like Haleem, strongly argue that is it a myth propagated by western scholars, 'some of who imagine that Muslims have nothing to fall back on except the decisions of the schools of law and scholars of the classical period' (MCB 2002). He believes that scholars in Muslim countries reach their own decisions on new situations based on the Qur'an and *ahadith*, without feeling bound by the conclusions of any earlier school of law.

Over time, other scholars have argued for the restoration of *ijtihad* as the means for rejuvenating Muslim civilisation. The whole debate is clearly put into context by Ramadan (1994) who cogently argues the case for a modern interpretation based upon the key sources. The restoration movement itself gathered pace over 200 hundred years ago. Mohammed Abduh's sentiments have a surprisingly modern ring to them. He was extremely critical of knowledge acquired by heart without any concern for interpretation and understanding. 'The tradition of memorising, he argued, if it had had some benefit, was no more able to fit our modern era for which we need, in addition to the religious matter, analytical knowledge, comprehension, and moreover, contextualisation' (Ramadan, 1994). This is not just an esoteric debate. It goes to the very heart of western Muslim people's attempts to locate themselves as western Muslims, and to the pedagogical style that many Muslims undergo at the madrasahs.

Madrasahs

Madrasah literally means a place of study. They are often referred to as mosque schools, though not all are attached to mosques. Some charge a small fee to cover basic costs but many are, in effect, subsidised by their communities. In Britain, they evolved as immigrants of Islam origin wanted to retain their faith and felt that mainstream schools were unable and often unwilling to provide the type of religious education they wanted for their children. Their curricula and pedagogy were time honoured and were modelled upon what they were used to in their country of origin. Teachers were and sometimes still are brought from those countries to provide the instruction. Given that the majority of Britain's Muslim youth are likely to attend madrasahs until they are at least fourteen, there is surprisingly little material available for well researched comment. Chapter 7 of the *RAISE project*, 'Being a British Muslim – linking with imams, mosques and madrasahs' (Richardson and Wood, 2004) contains the results of a small scale research project in Leicester City and some advice about bringing the various sectors together, but this is the exception rather than the rule.

It has long been a source of worry to mainstream educators that quite young children spend so much time after school in these institutions. Little know-ledge exists about the qualifications of the teachers in the madrasahs. Some are likely to be *ulama* who have attended *Darul Ulums* for a long time and have received qualifications. Others will be *hafiz* who have memorised the whole Qur'an by heart. Some will be volunteers, perhaps with little or no training.

The teachers generally teach pupils to learn the Qur'an, normally by heart, and inform them about the life of the Prophet and some of the fundamental teachings and practices of the Muslim way of life. Some pupils will learn about Muslim law and history. Some teach the basics of Arabic. The most innovative, however, encourage debate about what it means to be a Muslim at this time in the UK. The Nasiha project, for example, is a joint project be-tween the Council for Mosques Bradford (CFMB) and SERCO. It is a web-based tool for educating young Muslims on aspects of citizenship, which is interwoven around character teaching from the Islamic tradition. The Nasiha curriculum aims to embed good teaching exercises in madrasahs and help young Muslims to know their sacred roles and responsibilities in the societies we live and interact in (www.nasiha.co.uk).

It seems that, generally, the teaching style in the madrasahs is teacher directed; rote learning oriented, and does not encourage discourse, argu-ment, debate and interpretation. The *khutbah* (sermons) in mosques on Fridays follow a similar pattern; often declamatory in style, they are not intended to be conducive to discussion. Muslims pupils have little oppor-tunity to discuss the Qur'an, the *Sunnah* and *ahadith*. This difference in style can cause behavioural problems, especially for pupils who experience a totally different experience in mainstream schools. Although many LAs have provided a little funding to support these out-of-hours school experiences, there have been few attempts to bring mainstream and madrasahs together.

This is beginning to change, however. Concerted efforts by national and local government are seeking to support the training, resource provision and accreditation not just of those who teach in madrasahs but in the comple-mentary/supplementary sector generally. This is a crucial development for it provides LA recognition to a sector that has hitherto received little support. It also allows mainstream educators to influence the pedagogy of these institutions. Birmingham LA, for example, has developed a comprehensive package of training and accreditation for all interested parties. This is supported by a website and by a supplementary schools forum, where teachers and administrators can make their views known to the local authority.

Leicester City, supported by the School Development Support Agency (SDSA) has established an effective Leicester Complementary Schools Trust and in April 2006 held a very successful conference specifically aimed at madrasahs. The trust's report, *A Way Forward for Madrasahs* (www.lcst.org.uk) highlights the willingness of madrasahs to work closely with mainstream schools and indicates the support and guidance that madrasahs require. These include help with teaching and learning techniques, curriculum development, accreditation, and child protection. Most recently the SDSA are leading on the Islam and Citizenship Education Project (ICE).

Kirklees Local Authority in 2003 published their *Safe Children – Sound Learning Guidance for Madrasahs*. This was written as a result joint work on the 'Madressah Project' between the Lifelong Learning and Social Affairs and Health departments. The publication, aimed at the 50 madrasahs and supplementary schools throughout the authority, includes straightforward and accessible guidance on behaviour management, child protection, roles and responsibilities, health and safety and recruitment and training. It provides a comprehensive overview on most issues related to effective complementary schooling.

Dialogue and closer links generally with madrasahs are crucial, for attendance is a obligatory and fundamental part of a Muslim child's culture and identity. Mainstream schools need to capitalise on this form of out of hours provision so that the overall learning experience and hopefully attainment of the pupils is enhanced. In this they are supported by the National Resource Centre for Supplementary Education, a national body run by ContinYou, who are working with the whole supplementary sector but are planning a number of specific projects designed to support madrasahs (www. supplementary education.org.uk). Local Government is also increasingly recognising that madrasahs could play an important part in helping to raise the attainment of underachieving groups, and support the identities, cultures and religions of young people.

Developing the young British Muslim voice
The latest census figures reveal that a third of all British Muslims are between 0-15 years old, and another 18 per cent are aged 16-24. It is one of the

youngest minority ethnic and faith populations. For well over a decade, both central and local government have supported schools and colleges in strengthening democratic processes, and in enhancing children's and young people's active participation in them. Involving children and young people, particularly those who rarely have the opportunity to have a say, such as hard to reach groups and the socially excluded, can enhance their belief in their own ability to change and help them gain greater control over their own lives. A plethora of government inspired and other documents provide a statutory rationale and non-statutory guidance for the increased involvement of young people. *Hear by Right, Act by Right, the United Nations convention on the rights of the child,* and *Making a Positive Contribution* provide help and guidance to schools and authorities in progressing this participation agenda.

The Russell Commission, A National Framework for Youth Action and Engagement (2005) is equally explicit: 'the Commission's vision is of a society in which young people feel connected to their communities, seek to exercise influence over what is done and the way it is done, and are able to make a difference by having meaningful and exciting opportunities to volunteer.' Russell's framework offers a step change in young people's civic engagement and aims to make volunteering a common feature in their lives. Russell's research found that young people were clear that they wanted volunteering to have a tangible impact upon the communities in which they live. 'The key theme for the Commission is the importance of involving young people themselves in the design and implementation of volunteering activity ... for some of the most successful and inspirational volunteering experiences are those led by young people.'

As we have seen, faith is the key determinant in the lives of Muslims, and Islamic faith in action requires participation. All the available evidence indicates that young Muslims are keen to be part of this agenda. Many LAs have developed Youth Strategies and are undertaking a rethink of the role and function of their Youth workers, Youth Forums and Young People's Councils/ Youth Parliaments. Other LAs are creating shadow SACREs. Increasingly, young people are taking control of their own destinies.

Leicester's *Youth Voice*, though not exclusively Muslim, is an excellent example of a young people's organisation (for those aged between 18 and 24) that has taken control of its own agenda, sought and won the Neighbourhood Renewal Fund (NRF) and other funding and is now a limited company. Similarly, Birmingham's *Young Citizens* (15-25 years) address a range of social and political issues. Young Citizens is a multi-faith group with many Muslim leading lights. If young Muslims are seen as part of the problem, they must be part of the solution. They must be at the heart of the development of any new strategic approach to education and Islam.

Towards a new strategy

The major reasons why the education system must move towards a new strategy that deals with Muslims in education are outlined below. Perhaps the adjective 'new' is a misnomer as it is doubtful whether the education system has ever had an old one. The rationale, however, is clear: if faith is the key determinant of Muslim pupils' lives and identities, and if the key vehicle for accessing faith is revealed and acquired knowledge, then it follows that the Education system, the QCA, schools, Local Authorities, their many agencies and partners, and Further and Higher Education Institutions must take steps to understand more deeply the key components and issues for Muslim pupils. This deeper understanding must lead to effective strategies and real action in all areas of educational life, so that both Muslims and non-Muslims can begin to understand the contribution of Islam to our shared histories and the major issues that face British Muslims today, in terms of local, national and international contexts. National and local government departments, Health Authorities, LAs and schools – mainstream, independent and complementary – must engage in robust dialogue that leads to the formulation of a new strategy.

The fifteen key strategic components of the new approach to Islam

There are no easy answers or quick fixes to issues that have their roots deep in our shared histories and narratives. The keys are mutual understanding and dialogue. The development and implementation of a new strategy and the weighting given to its components will vary from institution to institution but there are some generic actions that are applicable in various degrees to everybody. Everyone involved with education, therefore, should:

1   seek and empathise with greater understanding that goes beyond the daily practices and rules of Islam to an awareness of the centrality of the love and remembrance of God in Islam, and of the major issues faced by British Muslim pupils, their parents and their communities

2   map current practices and expertise that relate to meeting the needs of Muslim pupils and tackling Islamophobia

3   discover and disseminate the good practice that already exists in many schools and institutions, and on the many websites dedicated to Islamic issues

4   devise strategies that are dedicated to closing the attainment gap and raising the self esteem of Muslims as Muslims

5   build these strategies into all major plans at school, local authority and central government levels

6   draw up and implement an overarching strategy, 'Islam and Education', that relates to all departments

7   ensure that all race equality and community cohesion policies address meeting the needs of Muslim pupils and countering Islamophobia

8   insist that all providers of Continuing Professional Development build the Islamic perspective into their courses, conferences, coaching and mentoring wherever applicable

9   support and help develop the complementary sector and build effective links with mainstream schools

10 support and help schools to provide consistent and coherent support to help their Muslim pupils grow up as 'good Muslims'

11 use Islamic values such as justice, compassion and service and the Islamic view of learning to motivate students

12 use the unique contributions that Islam has made to learning to raise students' self-esteem

13 encourage the development of curriculum materials and perspectives that reflect Muslim contributions to the contemporary world

14 encourage Muslims in their debate about what it means to be a British Muslim today

15 help build the capacity of young British Muslims to articulate and develop their own discourse, frame of reference and solutions

Some organisations, working singly or collectively, may wish to appoint an individual or individuals with specific responsibility for Muslim affairs. Others will seek to add it on to existing responsibilities. Some will seek funding from external sources to support the development and implementation of such a strategy. Others may use existing funds. Either way, the strategy will be need to monitored and evaluated as part of the normal institutional arrangements. There are some key process points, however, that all involved organisations would do well to consider.

Recommended processes for underpinning the development, implementation and evaluation of a new strategic approach

The new strategic approach is a dialogical and dialectical process. It is a two way process that encourages Muslims and non-Muslims to question, to become reflective, to examine Muslim views of the education service as it stands. Similarly, it encourages the education service to examine its own attitudes to Islam. There are no easy answers, no straightforward one size fits all. It will not be a comfortable or easy journey and many of the questions and challenges will emerge as the process develops.

The basic principles succinctly outlined by Michael Fullan (2001) perfectly cohere with the strategic analysis. He could be describing Islam and education when he writes that, 'the big problems of the day are complex, rife with paradoxes and dilemmas. For these problems there are no once-and-for all answers. Yet we expect our leaders to provide solutions' (Fullan, 2001). The five components of leadership that Fullan identifies resonate with my argument:

- leaders must act with moral purpose, with the intention of making a positive difference to the lives of pupils and society; and that moral purpose is normally accompanied by a sense of urgency

- leaders must understand the change process

- relationships, relationships relationships are the essential prerequisite for all effective change, and we now need to pay as much attention to how we treat people – the pupils, the parents, and the communities – as we typically pay to structures, strategies and statistics

- knowledge creation and sharing, turning information into knowledge is a social process, and for that you need good relationships

- coherence making is a key leadership function but that the nature of leadership must change. For Fullan, 'the leader becomes a context setter, the designer of a learning experience – not an authority figure with solutions'

This essentially means that we must involve in open non-prejudicial discourse the complete range of interested parties, with Heads, Directors and local government officers acting in partnership as the context setters. This would mean that we proactively

- involve Muslim communities
- involve parents and governors

■ involve madrasahs and mosques
■ involve pupils, Youth Voice and Student Councils
■ involve Community Cohesion and youth workers
■ involve Higher and Further Education Institutions

Conclusion

One could be forgiven for thinking that this new strategic approach with Every Muslim Child Matters at its heart is too large, too complex and too fraught with problems to begin even to contemplate. The experience and practices of the UK education system and its partners, which have success-fully undertaken so many major changes in recent years, however, gives great cause for optimism. Add to this the fact that, in spite of direct and institu-tional racism and the rising levels of Islamophobia, Muslims are free to prac-tise their religion, debate and argue, pray, build and attend mosques, under-take the pilgrimage and bear witness to God, gives even more cause for hope. Overlay this with a national characteristic which supports cultural change within its democratic and tolerant framework and you could conclude that if ever there was a society which could achieve the changes that would make it the paradigm of a multi-faith, multicultural, multiethnic world, then it is here and now in the UK. The adoption by all parties of the new strategic approach to Islam and education could well become a significant step towards the equality for which we all strive.

There is no better way than to end with the words that form the Prophet Muhammad's (PBUH) final sermon, words that underpin the essence of this strategy:

> People, verily your Lord and Sustainer is one and your ancestor is one. All of you descend from Adam and Adam was made of earth. There is no superiority for an Arab over a non-Arab nor for a non-Arab over an Arab; neither a white man over a black man nor a black man over a white man except the superiority gained through God consciousness. Indeed the noblest of you is the one who is most deeply con-scious of God. (*From the farewell sermon of the noble Prophet, delivered in Arafat and Mina in the month of Dhu'l-Hijjah 10 AH/630 CE*) (Muslim Council of Britain *The Quest for Sanity – Reflections on September 11th and the Aftermath 2002*)

2

Muslims and Cultural Inclusivity:
The quiet curriculum revolution

'The traditional approach to covering the syllabus has been exhausted; it has delivered all it can; it will work no more.' So said Ken Boston, Chief Executive of the Qualifications and Curriculum Authority (QCA), as he launched the new secondary curriculum in July 2007. The launch of this new curriculum with its revisions to twelve Key Stage 3 programmes of study, developments in eight Key Stage 4 and three new non-statutory programmes, marked the culmination of one period of extensive consultation across all phases into the nature of a curriculum for the 21st century. It formed one part of a quiet revolution that is underway in the world of curriculum development, a revolution that could and should have a profound effect all those involved in curriculum delivery: the school workforce, governors, and all those involved in training. It should have an equally profound effect upon the pupils and students. It is the gradual loosening of the received wisdom that schools were constrained by the national curriculum, were unable to think and operate outside the schemes of work, and were shackled by over prescription imposed by the Qualification and Curriculum Authority.

As Mick Waters, the QCA's Director of Curriculum eloquently put it (www.tes.co.uk June 8 2007): 'Schools are finally getting the confidence to make the curriculum work for them, rather than being slaves to something they imagine is the driver'. This shift, he argued, is a sign that schools want to organise their curriculum in a way that appeals to pupils. The sentiment behind this statement is, of course, that much of the curriculum presently on offer has limited appeal to young people. The Aiming High National Strategies – both those designed for pupils of African-Caribbean heritage and

41

MEAP (Minority Ethnic Achievement Project – have over time, and with some success, addressed the curricular and pedagogic needs of many of our under-achieving minority ethnic groups, including Muslim groups.

This secondary curriculum review forms part of the QCA's broader vision to develop a modern world class curriculum that will inspire and challenge all learners and prepare them for the future. The QCA Futures team, led by Mick Waters, were charged with the deceptively simply worded remit of developing a world class curriculum, and with helping schools refresh and renew their curriculum by, amongst other things:

- embedding the curriculum aims to help pupils become successful learners, confident individuals and responsible citizens

- improving coherence, highlighting commonalities between the key concepts at the heart of each subject, encouraging links between areas of curriculum and reducing the overall level of prescription

- making learning more relevant by linking it to the world beyond the classroom and to the *Every Child Matters* outcomes

In addition, the team were required to take into account changes in society and the nature of work, technological developments, new understandings about learning, the need for greater personalisation and innovation, and the increasing international dimension for life and work (www.qca.org.uk/futures).

These challenges are relevant to all groups, but changes in society, the need for greater personalisation, and the increasing international dimension will have particular resonance for Muslim pupils. The Futures Team traversed the country consulting teachers, governors, pupils and the world of work in a number of structured curriculum conversations. As a result of these conversations the QCA revised the aims of the curriculum, arguing that it should enable all young people to become:

- successful learners who, enjoy learning, make progress and achieve and (particularly relevant to Muslims) 'know about big ideas and events that shape our world'

- confident individuals who are able to live safe, healthy and fulfilling lives and (particularly relevant to Muslims) have secure values and have principles to distinguish right from wrong

- responsible citizens who make a positive contribution to society and (particularly relevant to Muslims) respect others and act with integrity, challenge injustice, are committed to human rights and strive to live peaceably with others. Young people, and particularly Muslim pupils, also need to understand their own and others' cultures and traditions, within the context of British Heritage, and have a strong sense of their own place in the world.

Over time the QCA has developed *A Big Picture of the Curriculum* which, because the curriculum cannot remain static but must be responsive to changes in society, will only ever be a working draft. The December 2007 version graphically illustrates the breath and depth of the curriculum as an entire planned learning experience. That experience (www.qca.org.uk) takes place in the normal school day, extended hours and out of school. For Muslims the out of school provision and its relationship to mainstream schooling are particularly relevant. Muslims between the ages of 4 and 14 spend a great deal of time at the mosque or madrasah learning. The major question is how this learning should relate to what they do in the normal school day, in terms of both content and of pedagogy.

An increasing number of schools are using the big picture of the curriculum as a stimulus tool in order to examine their own curriculum. For Muslim pupils issues of knowledge and understanding, of personal, social and emotional development are crucial. Similarly, the overarching significant themes like cultural diversity, identity and belonging are paramount to young British Muslims, who have to juggle the complex issues of their cultural and ethnic heritage, sometimes overlaid with race, and the possible hostility to their Islamic faith. For them the drive to increase personalisation has enormous implications. Ken Boston argues that

> The new curriculum' is designed to enable the personalisation of learning in a way the previous curriculum did not. While still prescribing the fundamental body of knowledge, skill and understanding that must form the core curriculum diet of all young people – using the heritage of the past to prepare them for future – it has depth and range necessary to enable teachers to focus their teaching on what each individual needs in order to progress. (www.qca.org.uk)

As we have argued, Islam is the key determinant in the lives of many Muslims in the UK. The new curriculum with its personalised, local and global perspectives allows and implicitly encourages schools to ensure that pupils are no longer required to leave their religion at home as they enter through the school portals. Mainstream secular schools with significant numbers of Muslim pupils can design a curriculum that supports the centrality of Islam in the life of its Muslim pupils by effectively utilising that fundamental body of knowledge, skills and understanding that form the core curriculum diet and by attempting to ensure synergy between mainstream school provision and that which is offered outside.

However, schools face two major problems in designing such a curriculum. The first relates to the culture of schools, which is generally not geared for curriculum development. The second relates to assessment that is not fit for the purpose of supporting the needs of Muslim pupils. Pete Chilvers (2004) outlines what he calls 'school improvement schizophrenia and parallel lives.'

Chilvers provides a fascinating narrative of the key drivers for school improvement in the 1990s. These drivers encouraged schools to raise educational standards by narrowly concentrating upon the tested and inspected aspects of the national curriculum whilst at the same time, as the decade wore on, exhorting teachers to be less prescriptive and more creative in their curriculum approaches. Chilvers concluded that

> we had created a generation of teachers who rarely considered it part of their professional duty, interest or pleasure, to develop curriculum content.

His analysis of the government's changing position and their use of language and concepts like 'informed professionalism' and 'earned autonomy' led him to believe that schools had a timely opportunity to develop what he called a culturally inclusive curriculum, a curriculum that could be built upon the rigour and organisation of existing plans and schemes of work that fulfil requirements, but can also be constructed and delivered according to the best principles of learning. 'In a nutshell we have the opportunity to create the National Inclusive Curriculum that situates learning at the level of values and identity.'

For Chilvers, a culturally inclusive curriculum is one that specifically prepares pupils for active participation in a culturally diverse society. It not only reflects the experiences of members of that society but also provides *all* pupils with knowledge, skills, attitudes and understanding that will empower and enable rather than inhibit them, as they make choices about living within that diverse society. Cultural inclusion is not exclusively a Muslim issue – it applies for all pupils. However, wherever the culture of school life is significantly different from pupils' home and community experiences, progress and attainment are likely to be impeded unless schools work proactively to meet the challenges and opportunities that these diverse experiences present. Developing a culturally inclusive curriculum is one instance of such proactive behaviour.

The language of the QCA new curriculum is slightly different, but the sentiments are exactly the same. To support schools in creating a culture that encourages school based curriculum development, QCA has pioneered a curriculum co-development approach which 'involves schools developing their curriculum to best meet the needs and interests of their learners, in partnership with others who challenge, offer support, listen, learn and help make connections.' (www.qca.org.uk/futuresinaction) Their curriculum co-development toolkit provides a range of structured activities and resources to help schools develop and improve their curriculum. It focuses on three key curriculum questions:

- *What* are you trying to achieve for your learners through the curriculum?

- *How* can you best organise learning to enable you to achieve your aims for your learners?

- *How* will you know when you have achieved your aims?

One of the earliest co-development networks involved nine schools in the East Midlands region and developed from their annual regional Advanced Skills Teachers (AST) conferences. Entitled, *ASTs as Curriculum Innovators*, supported by QCA and managed by the SDSA (www.sdsa.net), the project encouraged participants to devise, develop and evaluate a curriculum project in their own school. All participants came together for a day before and after the development to action plan, to present and extrapolate the key learning points. The processes and learning points are generic and can be applied to any situation. They will resonate, however, with any school that wants to develop a more inclusive curriculum for its Muslims pupils. Colleagues from the nine schools agreed that the key features of successful curriculum development were that:

- it was a journey: although there were precise outcomes, the processes involved a range of stakeholders, twists and turns that pragmatically led to changes in design, and that the whole was developmental

- it must proactively involve pupils: they become its most powerful advocates and critics

- it must proactively involve both teaching and support staff. Some of them may change over time and may be more or less actively involved at various times, but their commitment was crucial

■ it must proactively involve parents: this, depending on intended out-come, might prove fundamental to the project's success

■ it needs to be structurally and systematically supported: the support of senior managers was crucial but so was the allocation of time and resources

■ it needs to be well planned and embedded as part of the school routines. Sequential planning, not bolt-on one-offs was essential for both development and sustainability

■ it must have clear intended outcomes as a pre-requisite for success

■ it required a small dedicated team of key workers who had planned meeting dates, times, patterns of work. This was necessary to retain impetus and focus

■ it required allocated time for training of staff and for research and development

If schools decide to develop a curriculum that better suits the needs of their Muslim pupils, how will they know if the curriculum changes have made a difference? How will they know if they have achieved their aims? The team that worked on a DfES research project which became known as CREAM (the Curriculum Reflecting the Experiences of African Caribbean and Muslim pupils – www.sdsa.net) developed thirteen generic criteria they called the 'Curriculum Big Ideas', that can be used with reference to any cultural needs. They were employed to excellent effect by Oldham LEA as part of their whole school secondary project and have been used to develop curriculum thinking in relation to pupils of multiple heritage. They are illustrated here with Muslim examples:

Meeting the needs of Muslim pupils: cultural inclusion criteria
1 commonalities
Does the curriculum stress, at the same time that it depicts diversity of culture and experience, that all people share common aspirations, needs and concerns by virtue of their humanity? For example, does it teach about similarities and common humanity when depicting aspects of British Muslim culture and experience?

2 diverse perspectives
Does the curriculum teach that there are a variety of perceptions, inter-pretations and perspectives with regard to every event? For example, does

it teach about perceptions, outlooks and experiences of British Muslim people?

3 diversity within diversity

Does the curriculum counteract over-simplified, stereotypical views by teaching that, within every cultural tradition, there is a diversity of viewpoints, lifestyle and beliefs? For example, does it show that there are many differences within Muslim culture and experience?

4 narratives

Does the curriculum teach that every culture interprets its history and learning through certain grand narratives and that these, in turn, contribute to the identities of individuals? For example, does it depict key narratives in Muslim cultures?

5 multiple identities

Does the curriculum teach that most people have a range of affiliations, loyalties and sense of belonging? For example, does it illustrate that all of us, and maybe especially Muslim pupils from ethnic minority backgrounds, assume different roles and behaviour patterns within different settings and readily switch between them?

6 status and credibility

Does the curriculum give status to the experiences and achievement of people from all backgrounds and cultures in terms that pupil's value? For example, is the point of comparison just with the dominant Anglo culture or does the curriculum also acknowledge Muslim and other perspectives?

7 racism

Does the curriculum teach about issues of racism, for example distinctions between colour racism and cultural racism and between personal and institutional, and about ways of preventing and addressing racism? Does it help Muslim pupils to deal with issues of Islamophobia?

8 interdependence and borrowing

Does the curriculum teach that all learning and human achievement is dependent upon the prior learning and achievement of others and often builds upon and borrows from other cultural traditions? For example, does history teaching recognise how much scientific knowledge commonly attributed to Renaissance discovery was actually an evolutionary development of earlier Islamic thinking?

9 positive role models

Does the curriculum depict people from a range of cultures and backgrounds achieving eminence as inventors, entrepreneurs, leaders and artists, and demonstrating creativity, initiative and moral courage? For example, are Muslim pioneers and achievers given a place of significance?

10 normal not exotic

Does the curriculum show that diversity is an aspect of contemporary experience and ordinary daily life, not merely a feature of distant lands? For example, do pupils learn about everyday Muslim experience in Britain today?

11 excellence everywhere

Does the curriculum teach that excellence is not restricted to the achievements of people within dominant cultures, but that people in all cultures, today and in the past, achieve excellence?

12 inclusion

Does the curriculum specifically promote a culture of inclusion, teaching that all people of all cultures and backgrounds are of equal value and their ideas equally worthy of consideration?

13 dynamic culture

Does the curriculum teach that societies and the cultures within them are constantly changing and developing? Does it teach that there is not a fixed, static view or perspective for a cultural group in any time or place? For example, is the demography of Britain studied to show how, throughout history and today, British identity is shaped by the constant flow of people and ideas? Does it teach that Islam itself, whilst remaining true to its core values, has evolved over time in different contexts and that the perceptions of British Muslims might be very different from those, for example, of their Arab cousins?

These criteria form one part of an assessment process designed to help schools in their curricular quest. Another and equally valuable tool is, what Chilvers has called, 'the Islameter'. School self-evaluation activities have become quite well established in British schools over recent years. Indeed, the latest phase of Ofsted school inspection is built extensively upon a thorough self evaluation routine (the SEF) carried out within schools on an ongoing basis. In making evaluative judgments, schools are becoming accustomed to making comparisons against pre-written descriptors of work, and to describe development, implementation and enhancement.

Typically speaking, these stage descriptors provide four developmental steps:

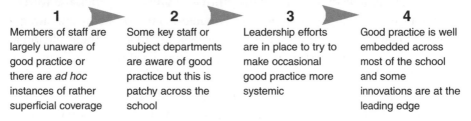

1	2	3	4
Members of staff are largely unaware of good practice or there are *ad hoc* instances of rather superficial coverage	Some key staff or subject departments are aware of good practice but this is patchy across the school	Leadership efforts are in place to try to make occasional good practice more systemic	Good practice is well embedded across most of the school and some innovations are at the leading edge

A hugely useful (free!) interactive tool to support schools with self evaluation activities is available online at (http://matrix.becta.org.uk). Two examples can be found under the inclusion subheading. This site leads users through a series of comparative judgments and then provides action planning suggestions to move the situation forward. It uses a four stage framework similar to the chart above. Schools should review their curriculum provision to examine the extent to which it reflects Muslim experience. This evaluation could be structured in a worthwhile manner by applying the same four stage analysis – using the Islameter.

The Islameter

1	2	3	4
Most of staff are unaware of opportunities to reflect Muslim experience	Some key staff are aware of some opportunities to reflect Muslim experience	Leadership efforts are in place to try to make such opportunities part of school policy	Opportunities to reflect Muslim experience are well embedded across most of the school

By applying a simple measure of the extent to which the curriculum reflects Islamic experience, schools can find their most relevant starting points for developing culturally inclusive approaches with respect to Muslim issues.

The following sections provide some practical support for schools that might choose to use this approach. It is based upon some of the findings of the CREAM research, the excellent work of the Muslim Heritage consultancy, and the Foundation for Science and Technology, and a thorough review of all the new programmes of study for Key Stage 3 and 4, undertaken as part of the QCA funded CUSP project (Cultural Understandings in Science).

The curriculum: highlighting opportunities and resources to reflect the Muslim experience and heritage

We have examined some of the key drivers and rationale that underpin the quiet curriculum revolution inspired by the QCA. The new curriculum with its personalised, local and global perspectives allows and implicitly encourages schools to ensure that pupils are no longer required to leave their religion at home when they come to school. Mainstream secular schools with significant numbers of Muslim pupils can design a curriculum that supports and effectively utilises the centrality of Islam in the life of its Muslim pupils. We have also outlined the criteria that schools might wish to use to develop their own inclusive big curriculum picture and offered a simple Islameter against which they can assess their own progress.

The issue of teacher knowledge and confidence in dealing with Islamic matters, and resource availability still remains however. In 2003 the DfES commissioned a major piece of research 'to establish the extent and quality of materials reflecting the experience of African Caribbean and Muslim pupils that could be used by mainstream schools within the National Curriculum.' It became known as the CREAM report and was published by the SDSA on its website in 2004 (www.sdsa.net).

This report consisted of two related but discrete parts. The first, 'Methodology, Main Findings and Future Directions', summarised the how, the what, and the maybes of the project. The second, the 'Audit and the Materials' outlined areas that lend themselves directly or potentially to reflecting the experience of Muslim pupils, and offered lists of possible resources and practices that could support teachers. Members of the project team, and others who were commissioned to undertake particular subject-based aspects, conducted what is probably the most extensive materials search ever undertaken with reference to Muslim pupils. Their work established that over the years there has been almost no research regarding the position of Muslim pupils as Muslims, in the education system; neither was there much research concerning the dominant cultural groups that make up the Muslim communities, such as Pakistani and Bangladeshi heritage. No attempt had been made to map the curriculum against criteria designed to reflect their experiences. And there had been almost no curriculum development work in this area.

CREAM's overarching conclusions were optimistic but at the same time depressing. The report highlighted the many positive and committed attitudes revealed by LEA, school and community practitioners across the country. However, it demonstrated that in most areas of the curriculum the position relating to Muslim pupils generally is poor, with the exception of RE (which strictly speaking is not part of the National Curriculum), where it is strong. The unanimous view from all respondents was that this mapping exercise and audit of resources was desperately needed and everybody was very positive about the decision to explore Muslim experiences. Although much good work had already been undertaken in relation to the linguistic and cultural needs of underachieving groups like Bangladeshis and Pakistanis, colleagues strongly felt that a generic concentration on their curriculum experiences as adherents of Islam was a significant step.

In recent years many LEAs had concentrated on the wider issues of race equality and had produced excellent packs to support their schools. These tended to concentrate on issues of leadership and management, and of policy and strategy. They generally lacked detail and depth in terms of curriculum planning and classroom organisation and management. Nor did they offer resources that might be used to support the experiences of Muslim projects.

The CREAM report concluded that although individual LEAs and sections of government departments have produced projects and materials, it was not coherent, not joined-up and not effectively disseminated. There was nothing that approached a coherent strategy. Materials were hard to find and hard to access. Some library services, however, offered a comprehensive trawl on books and materials, sometimes with brief commentaries – although teachers have to adapt them.

The major issue identified by respondents was the lack of curriculum development over some years, which had led to a recycling of earlier material, much of it now dated. The report concluded that a system that relies on the enthusiasm of individual schools, teachers and LEAs will not produce an effective curriculum that reflects the experiences and heritage of Muslim pupils. There are pockets of good practice, often financed by various DfES projects. The QCA have undertaken some limited work in their *Respect for All* projects, but there is little effective joined up thinking between the various government financed organisations like DCSF, QCA, TDA and EHRC (Equality and Human Rights Commission). It is probably true to say that the CREAM report had some influence on the government's decision to extend their Aiming High strategy into other underachieving groups like Bangladeshi, Pakistani, Turkish and Somali pupils. This successful project became known as MEAP (Minority Ethnic Achievement Project).

The new secondary curriculum

A year after CREAM, the government decided to launch its review of the secondary curriculum, the results of which herald a new era for curriculum development. A small QCA booklet *'The New Secondary Curriculum: What has Changed and Why?* (available from www.qca.org.uk) provides an overview of what has changed the opportunities for schools and the support available. The new curriculum has been based upon extensive consultation which included general discussion about the nature of curriculum requirements in the 21st century and specific consultation on revisions and inclusions to the programmes of study at Key Stage 3 and Key Stage 4. As their launch booklet states

> such a range of reforms rarely comes at one time and we need to seize the opportunity to make a lasting difference. A high-quality national framework has been established: now schools have a unique opportunity to build upon their own curriculum that reflects the local context and meets their learners' needs, capabilities and aspirations.

The revised programmes of study share a common and useful format:

- **an importance statement** describes the important aspects of the subject, explains what learners can expect to gain from studying it and identifies how it links to the aims of the curriculum

- **key concepts** identify the main areas that learners need to understand in order to deepen and broaden their knowledge, skills and understanding. Many of the programmes of study include a key section on cultural understanding

- **key processes** identify the essential skills and processes that students need to make progress in their subject

- **range and content** outlines the breadth of subject matter from which teachers should draw when teaching the key concepts and processes

- **curriculum opportunities** identify opportunities to enhance learners' engagement with the subject

The implications of these changes are profound for all pupils. A key feature of the reforms is that there will be less prescribed content and far more teacher and learner autonomy. The QCA will continue to provide support and curriculum guidance to schools and, over time will examine the schemes of work. Until this happens, however, it is likely that teachers will continue to use the schemes of a work as their key reference point and it is for this reason that an amended and updated version of aspects of CREAM has been produced. The major problem has been that, hitherto, teachers generally used the schemes not merely as guidance, as originally intended, but in many cases as a device for ensuring compliance, so teachers were often reluctant to move away from them.

The authors of the CREAM report decided to map provision against the Early Years Goals and QCA Schemes of Work Key Stage 1-3, rather than the programmes of study, as these were the predominant point of reference for most curriculum planning and delivery. Their extensive mapping exercise revealed that there were some areas where there was great potential to reflect the experience and heritage of Muslim pupils, and an enormous number of others with considerable potential, but which might need preparatory work to contextualise learning, match appropriate resources, or even rewrite key elements.

The remainder of this chapter considers the opportunities and resources that reflect the Muslim experience and heritage on a subject by subject basis. They are based upon the original CREAM exercise, the MEAP experience, the original feedback on the draft programmes of study submitted by the Foundation for Science and Technology, and a thorough analysis of the new programmes of study at Key Stage 3 and 4. Much of the language of these new programmes is used in this text. The curriculum review and all programmes of study are available electronically from www.qca.org.uk. Art and Design and Music, however, are not included in this analysis as they form part of a discrete chapter in this book by Robert Bunting.

■ Citizenship

Citizenship throughout all key stages offers an excellent opportunity to reflect and develop Muslim experience and heritage. The revised programmes of study at Key Stage 3 and 4 are replete with exciting possibilities to introduce issues that are of genuine relevance and concern for so many young Muslims. As with so many areas, however, teacher search and selection is crucial to ensuring the embedding of the perspective. There are so many issues that are pertinent to Muslims and citizenship, but there is little available literature and few curriculum materials. The excellent Islamic Relief publication *Citizenship and Muslim Perspectives – Teachers Sharing Ideas* is the best in this area and provides a wealth of ideas and information. The citizenship curriculum is also the perfect vehicle for raising the issue of Islamophobia.

The 'general' potential within Citizenship to promote culturally inclusive values and Muslim perspectives can be depicted as follows:

Key Stage 1: Pupils learn about themselves as members of a community, with rights and responsibilities for themselves, for others and for their environment. They learn about their own and other people's feelings and become aware of the views, needs and rights of other children and older people. They begin to recognise that they have an active role to play in their community.

Key Stage 2: Pupils discuss and debate topical issues, including global problems and events. They learn to understand other people's experiences, to appreciate the range of religious and ethnic identities in the United Kingdom and to recognise and challenge stereotypes.

Key Stage 3 and 4: the new programmes of study are clear about the importance of citizenship,

> Citizenship encourages respect for different national, religious and ethnic identities. It equips pupils to engage critically with and explore diverse ideas, beliefs, and cultures and identifies the values we share as citizens in the UK. Pupils begin to understand how society has changed and is changing in the UK, Europe and the wider world ... pupils evaluate information, make informed judgments and reflect on the consequences of their actions now and in the future

The key concepts of democracy and justice encourage young people to consider how democracy, justice, diversity and toleration, respect and freedom are valued by people with different beliefs, backgrounds and traditions within a changing democratic society.

The section on 'identities and diversity: living together in the UK' includes four key components which are fundamental in highlighting the Muslim experience:

- appreciating that identities are complex, can change over time and are informed by different understandings of what it means to be a citizen in the UK

- exploring the diverse national, regional, ethnic and religious cultures, groups and communities in the UK and the connections between them

- considering the interconnections between the UK and the rest of Europe and the wider world

- exploring community cohesion and the different forces that bring about change in communities over time

The programmes of study include an introduction to the concept of 'multiple identities' and encourage analysis of common or shared identities. Such a vehicle is perfect for discussion of the *ummah*, and for the discussion of the differences between religious and cultural identities amongst Muslim youth. It also encourages debate about topical and controversial issues and problems which can lead to disagreement. These should not be avoided, but need to be handled so that pupils develop skills in discussing and debating citizenship issues and considering points of view that are not necessarily their own.

The range and content includes aspects of the changing nature of UK society, including the diversity of ideas, beliefs, cultures, identities, traditions, perspectives and values that are shared. It encourages discourse about migration to, from and within the UK and the reasons for this. Learning about diversity also involves recognising that culture, including the language, ideas and customs, traditions and religions practiced by people within a group, help constitute identity.

Curriculum opportunities include community based citizenship activities which could involve relationships with madrasahs and mosque committees; and campaigning – learning how to influence those in power particularly relevant to issues of concern like aspects of foreign policy or responses to controversial issues like the Danish cartoon of the Prophet Mohammad (PBUH).

Muslim potential within the QCA scheme of work for citizenship

Key Stage 1 and 2

These study units have great potential to directly reflect Muslim experience:

Unit 5	Living in a diverse world
Unit 7	Children's rights

These study units have considerable potential to reflect Muslim experience, but may need preparatory work to contextualise learning, match appropriate resources, or even rewrite key elements:

Unit 3	Animals and us
Unit 10	Local democracy and young citizens
Unit 11	In the media – what's the news?

55

Key Stage 3

These study units have great of potential to directly reflect Muslim experience:

Unit 3	Human rights
Unit 4	Britain – a diverse society?
Unit 9	The significance of the media
Unit 10	Debating a global issue
Unit 11	Difficulty in keeping world peace
Unit 17	School linking

These study units have considerable potential to reflect Muslim experience, but may need preparatory work to contextualise learning, match appropriate resources, or even rewrite key elements:

Unit 1	Citizenship – what's it all about?
Unit 6	Governments, election and voting
Unit 7	Local democracy
Unit 12	What's the point of voting today?
Unit 13	How do we deal with conflict?
Unit 14	Developing skills for democracy
Unit 15	Crime and safety awareness
Unit 16	Celebrating human rights
Unit 20	What's in the public interest?

Key Stage 4

These study units have great potential to directly reflect Muslim experience:

Unit 1	Human rights
Unit 3	Challenging racism, discrimination
Unit 12	Global issues, local action

Useful Muslim resources for citizenship

Books and Journals

Claire H (2001) *Not Aliens: Primary School Children and the Citizenship/PSHE Curriculum*. Stoke on Trent: Trentham

Osler A (2000) *Citizenship and Democracy in Schools: Diversity, identity, equality.* Stoke on Trent: Trentham

Runneymede Trust (2003) *Complementing Teachers.* London: LETTS Educational

See Food tasting and community links Chapter

Tide ~ DEC (2007) *Writing our Past.* Birmingham: Islamic Relief and Tide

Tide ~ DEC (2000) *Whose Citizenship? A Teacher's Toolkit.* Birmingham: Islamic Relief and Tide

Tide ~ DEC (2003) *Citizenship and Muslim Perspective – Teachers Sharing Ideas.* Birmingham: TIDE and Islamic Relief

Websites

Britkid
www.britkid.org (accessed August 2007)

Planet Teacher
The concept of Khalifa explains the Islamic view of responsibility for the environment
www.christian-aid.org.uk/learn/schools/secondary/freeitem/regcs/respl.pdf (August 2007)

QCA 'Respect for All'
http://www.qca.org.uk/qca_6753.aspx (August 2007)

Tide
http://www.tidec.org/index.html (August 2007)

The Global Express, (2007) DEP Manchester
http://www.dep.org.uk/ge/index.php (August 2007)

■ History

The History curriculum is a rich area of opportunity to develop a culturally in-clusive curriculum that reflects the experience and heritage of Muslim pupils. Within the QCA schemes of work there is just the one study unit in Key Stage 3 that has a specifically Muslim focus but many more that can be adapted to create a relevant focus and context. There are also a number of study units that could be rewritten fairly simply in a way that changes the content focus yet maintains balanced coverage of the historical skills of enquiry and fully contributes to the learning objectives within the scheme.

The new History programme of study at Key Stage 3 offers great potential to reflect Muslim experience and heritage. History helps pupils develop their own identities though gaining understanding of history at personal, local, national and international level. It helps them ask and answer questions of the present by engaging with the past. This is crucial for young British Mus-lims as they struggle to come to terms with the glories of their Islamic past, juxtaposed with the challenges of the present in order, perhaps, to fashion a British Muslim identity for the future.

Pupils find out about the history of their community, Britain, Europe and the world. They develop a chronological overview that enables them to make connections within and across different periods and societies. It encourages mutual understanding of the historic origins and cultural diversity, and helps pupils become confident and questioning individuals.

History provides all, including Muslim pupils, the opportunity to learn about the origins of the diversity of UK society. It also shows how past actions and choices have affected the environment and the quality of people's lives. It explains the motivation of individuals who made sacrifices for a particular cause and how events throughout history and around the world are inter-related. It can help pupils learn the causes of previous conflicts and the impacts they had, showing the importance of resolving conflict fairly.

To reflect Muslim experience well, history teaching and learning need to demonstrate how democracies have evolved in a range of societies and what we can learn from other forms of government. By focusing on the importance of intercultural understanding in the past and the implications of this today, pupils can begin to appreciate the different perspectives on events when seen from a range of standpoints. Many Muslim students in contemporary society are learning to reconcile the range of viewpoints that arise from their multiple identities, and a history curriculum that explores cultural perspectives on the interpretation of shared events will support their development. The historical antecedents of Islam live in the present time and it is important for young British Muslims to understand why historians have interpreted events in different and sometimes conflicting ways. As the Key Stage 3 programme of study puts it:

> People represent and interpret the past in many different ways, including in pictures, plays, films, reconstructions, museum displays, and fictional and non-fictional accounts. Interpretations reflect the circumstances in which they are made, the available evidence, and the intentions of those who make them

There is very little evidence, however, of curriculum materials that exemplify such work in schools. While there are generic materials that promote cultural diversity or take a black perspective, there is little that takes a distinctly Muslim experience into account. However, there is enormous potential within the schemes of work for the Muslim heritage to be exemplified.

Muslim potential within the QCA Scheme of Work for History
Key Stage 1 and 2

These study units have great potential to directly reflect Muslim experience and heritage:

Unit 13	Britain since 1948
Unit 16	Indus Valley civilization

These study units have considerable potential to reflect Muslim experience and heritage, but may need preparatory work to contextualise learning, match appropriate resources, or even rewrite key elements:

Unit 1	Toys today and in the past
Unit 2	What were homes like long ago?
Unit 6	Romans, Anglo Saxons, Vikings
Unit 8	Rich and poor in Tudor times
Unit 9	Children in WW2
Unit 10	Discovering Ancient Egypt
Unit 11	Children in Victorian Britain
Unit 12	Victorian changes in our locality

In addition, the following study units are identified as ones that could feasibly be re-written to reflect Muslim experience. Each of these study units have particular content that could simply be substituted for more contextual information and still meet the history learning objectives.

Unit 3	What were seaside holidays like in the past?
Unit 4	Why do we remember Florence Nightingale?
Unit 5	How do we know about the Great Fire of London?
Unit 7	Why did Henry VIII marry six times?
Unit 14	Who were the Ancient Greeks?
Unit 15	How do we use Ancient Greek ideas today?

Key Stage 3

These study units have great potential to directly reflect Muslim experience and heritage:

Unit 6	Islamic states 600 – 1600
Unit 13	Mogul India 1526 – 1857
Unit 14	The British Empire

These study units have considerable potential to reflect Muslim experience and heritage, but may need preparatory work to contextualise learning, match appropriate resources, or even rewrite key elements:

Unit 1	Introductory unit
Unit 2	Medieval monarchs
Unit 5	Elizabeth 1st tackling problems
Unit 7	Portraits 1500 -1750
Unit 8	The civil wars
Unit 9	Glorious revolution to the '45
Unit 10	France 1789 – 94
Unit 12	British middle class life in 1900
Unit 15	Black people of America
Unit 17	Divided Ireland
Unit 18	Hot war – cold war

In addition, the new programmes of study encourage the teaching of aspects of history including:

- the development of political power from the middle ages to the 20th century

- the impact through time of the movement and settlement of diverse peoples to, from, and within the British Isles. The examples used should help pupils reach an informed understanding of, and respect for, their own and each other's identities. This section provides an open invitation to include Islamic elements that were introduced into Britain and became part of its way of life and history. Issues about immigration can include the beginning of British multiculturalism. The use of oriental and Indian features in the Brighton Palace, the introduction of coffee houses and kiosks by Turkish merchants, the bath or *Hammam* and shampooing by Mohammed Sake, are a few examples which can help illuminate the changing nature of the United Kingdom.

- the ways in which lives, beliefs, ideas and attitudes of people in Britain have changed over time and the factors – such as technology, economic development, war religion and culture – that have driven theses changes. What, for example, has been the influence of Islamic belief and culture on the UK? Why are there now over 1.6 million Muslim in Britain?

- the development of trade, colonisation, industrialisation and technology, the British Empire. There could be a focus on the British empire and its effects both on Britain and the regions it colonised, as well as its legacy in the contemporary world, for example in the Middle East or the Indian sub-continent

- the changing nature of conflict and cooperation between countries and people and its lasting impact on national, ethnic, racial, cultural or religious issues

- links should be made to some of the parallel events changes and developments in British, European and world history. For example, a study of the political and cultural achievements of the Islamic states 600-1600 could provide a contrasting overview of the medieval period in Britain. In particular, the European period known as the Dark Ages could be effectively contrasted with the brilliance of Islamic society at the time and links should be made between the European renaissance and the great debt it owed to Islamic science, arts technology and culture generally

The curriculum should provide opportunities at Key Stage 3 for pupils to explore the ways in which the past has helped shape identities, shared cultures, values and attitudes today. It should also encourage them to investigate aspects of personal, family or local history and how they relate to a broader historical context. Pupils should also use ICT to research information about the past, process historical date, and select categories, organise and present their findings. This includes evaluating websites, considering the provenance of materials and assessing their value – a particularly important skill for Muslims who might be attracted to the more radical websites.

Useful Muslim resources for History
Books and journals

Claire H (1996) *Reclaiming our Pasts: Equality and Diversity in the Primary History Curriculum.* Stoke on Trent: Trentham

Hazareesingh S, Kenway and Simms (1994) *Speaking About the Past: Oral History for 5-7 year olds: A Resource for Teachers.* Stoke on Trent: Trentham

King A S and Reiss M (1993) *The Multicultural Dimension of the National Curriculum.* Oxford: Routledge Falmer

Visram R (1986) *Ayahs, Lascars and Princes – Indians in Britain 1700-1947.* London: Pluto

Visram R (1987) *Indians in Britain.* London: Batsford

Websites

The main web based sources can be accessed by using 'Black History Month' in an internet search. This will reveal a large number of sites, often with local information that can be sorted according to need. 'Black' history tends to be a generic term that covers black and Asian. It does not necessarily distinguish further in terms of Muslim issues. There are several sites that provide useful links to others. But few resources outline Muslim heritage and perspectives.

Ahmed Iqbal Ullah Race Relations Archive
See publications Breathing Space Black, Britain in the 20th Century, Britain since 1930, Refugee Experiences
http://www.racearchive.org.uk/ (August 2007)

Channel 4.com
www.channel4.com/history (August 2007)

Indus Valley KS2
www.harappa.com/teach (August 2007)

PCET Publishing
http://www.pcet.co.uk/ (August 2007)

The Journey
www.primarycolours.net (August 2007)

The Spread of Knowledge Game
www.muslimhomeschool.com/pride/edmaterial/Sharing.htm (August 2007)

The Virtual Classroom
www.virtualclassroom.org (August 2007)

Walsall LA
A study unit for KS3 based upon a comparison between the Tudors and the Mogul Empire (1500 -1700)
http://www.walsall.gov.uk/index.htm (August 2007)

■ Science

Since the original publication of the CREAM material (2004) the excellent *1001 Inventions* produced by the Foundation for Science Technology and Civilization (FSTC) (al Hassani, 2006) in conjunction with Muslim Heritage Consulting, and in collaboration with the Association of Science Education and consultants, have revolutionised the possibilities available for science teachers to incorporate the Muslim experiences and heritage into science teaching. Their exhibition, book, teachers guide and posters now provide a wonderful resource for teachers to directly incorporate these perspectives. And there is a range of useful websites, books and other resources which can be adapted to suit various sections of the science and history programmes of study. They tend not to be discrete but require sifting and organising to suit the lesson objectives. Likewise there are some books that provide help and advice; and again with the exception of *1001 Inventions*, there are few lesson plans available.

There are numerous situations within the science curriculum where the teacher selects resources, artefacts, materials, festivals, food or plants to enrich or illustrate their teaching. Such situations can sometimes afford the opportunity to select items that provide a reflection of Muslim experience within the teaching and learning.

Scientific enquiry is centred upon original and creative thinking and schools should seek to portray these processes as universal and global and not the exclusive domain of white, western men. An important role for curriculum materials can therefore be to illustrate the tremendous and increasingly recognised contribution to scientific discovery made by Islamic scholars in the past.

It is worth noting that the pursuit of knowledge is a sacred duty in Islam, not only as a way leading to the discovery of God but also as a means for the improvement of the quality of human life. Muslims of the Middle Ages made giant leaps forward in the area of science and Baghdad, Damascus, Cairo and Cordoba were cities at the centre of civilisation. The leading works of Ibn Al-Haytam (965-1039 CE) in optics, Jasbir Ibn Hayyan and Al-Razi (865-925) in chemistry, Al-Zahrawi (936-1013) in surgery, Al-Khawarizmi (780-850 CE) in Algebra and mathematics and Ibn Sina (980-1037) in medicine, and hundreds more Muslim scientists shaped modern science in such a way that Briffault (1928) acknowledged that science 'owes a great deal more to the Arab culture, it owes its existence'

Key Stage 1 and 2

These study units have considerable potential to reflect Muslim experience, but may need preparatory work to contextualise learning, match appropriate resources, or even rewrite key elements:

Unit 1a	Ourselves
Unit 2a	Health and growth
Unit 3a	Teeth and eating
Unit 3d	Rocks and soils
Unit 3e	Magnets and springs
Unit 3f	Light and shadows
Unit 5a	Keeping healthy
Unit 5e	Earth, sun and moon
Unit 6b	Micro-organisms
Unit 6f	How we see things

Selecting resources to support science teaching and learning

There are numerous situations within the science curriculum where the teacher selects resources, artefacts, materials, festivals, food or plants to enrich or illustrate their teaching. Such situations can sometimes give rise to the opportunity to select items that provide a reflection of Muslim experience within the teaching and learning.

The following tables, originally devised by Chilvers for the CREAM research, indicate potential areas within the QCA schemes of work to reflect Muslim pupils' experiences either by direct reference or by contextualisation.

Section 1.01 Unit 1A Ourselves		
Learning Objectives Children should learn:	**(i) Examples of possible teaching activities**	**Reference to curriculum materials**
that there are differences between humans	Amongst the range of data that can be collected within this unit, there is the opportunity to include skin colour. This data collection activity will need to link directly with learning about colour shades, preferred language, similarities and differences. A key question teachers may wish to ask is 'What colour are Muslims?' Followers of Islam are drawn from all ethnic groups, a large range of different cultures and consequently different skin colours. For example, in England there are white Muslims (often European), black Muslims (often African) and a large number of brown Muslims usually from south Asia.	

Section 1.02 Unit 2A Health and growth

Learning Objectives Children should learn:	(i) Examples of possible teaching activities	Reference to curriculum materials
that there are many different foods that we eat different kinds of food	Whether or not there are Muslim children in the class, this unit gives ideal opportunity to reflect the food experiences of families of many backgrounds. Activities and discussions could include similarities and differences, links to basic food groups, food for special occasions.	

Section 1.03 Unit 3A Teeth and eating

Learning Objectives Children should learn:	(i) Examples of possible teaching activities	Reference to curriculum materials
that an adequate and varied diet is needed to keep healthy	The suggested teaching activity within the QCA unit provides a direct opportunity to look at food from Islamic and other cultures, whether or not such diets are familiar to the children. It is also suggested that inviting guests into school could enhance the teaching about adequacy and variety. Care should be taken not to portray differences as exotic or unusual, especially in schools with a dominant monoculture.	

Section 1.04 Unit 3D Rocks and soils

Learning Objectives Children should learn:	(i) Examples of possible teaching activities	Reference to curriculum materials
that rocks are used for a variety of purposes	Include the use of different rocks within places of worship in Muslim and other faith buildings, both within the construction and the interior detail, e.g. the use of marble.	
that rocks are chosen for particular purposes because of their characteristics	Illustrate the effect created by the use of different stone within buildings in different places, e.g. Blue Mosque in Istanbul or the Taj Mahaal.	

Section 1.05 Unit 3F Light and Shadows

Learning Objectives Children should learn:	(i) Examples of possible teaching activities	Reference to curriculum materials
that shadows of objects in sunlight change over the course of the day	Create links between children's shadow stick experiments and the Muslim prayer times. *Fajr* (Dawn Prayer) takes place before sunrise. *Zuhr* (Noon Prayer) begins just after the sun has passed the meridian. Asr (Afternoon Prayer) begins when the length of the shadow of an object is	
that shadows change in length and position throughout the day	equal to the object's length plus the shadow's length at noon. *Maghrib* (Sunset Prayer) begins immediately after sunset. *Isha* (Night Prayer) begins when the sky is completely dark.	

Section 1.06 Unit 5A Keeping healthy

Learning Objectives Children should learn:	(i) Examples of possible teaching activities	Reference to curriculum materials
that to stay healthy we need an adequate and varied diet	One legacy of Greek science was nutritional theory about a balanced diet. This survived through the early Middle Ages of Europe in a somewhat threadbare form until it was further developed by the Islamic Moors of Spain and was revived early in the Renaissance period.	
that the muscle in the walls of the heart contracts regularly, pumping blood round the body	In the 10th century, Islam's Al-Razi wrote extensively about the venous system, accurately describing the function of the veins and their valves.	
that the blood vessels taking blood from the heart are called arteries and those returning it to the heart are called veins	In the 13th century Ibn An-Nafs and Ibn Al-Quff provided full documentation that blood circulates and correctly described the physiology of the heart and valves. This was 300 years before William Harvey was credited with these discoveries.	

Section 1.07 Unit 5E Earth, sun and moon

Learning Objectives Children should learn:	(i) Examples of possible teaching activities	Reference to curriculum materials
that the sun, earth and moon are approximately spherical that it is the earth that moves, not the sun, spinning on its axis once every 24 hours	Al-Biruni, a famous Muslim scholar in the 11th century, worked out that the earth is round and calculated its circumference. He also stated that the earth spins on its axis and rotates around the sun – 600 years before Galileo.	
that the earth takes a year to make one complete orbit of the sun, spinning as it goes	In the 15th century, Uligh Beg constructed a three-storey observatory in central Asia. The main instrument of the observatory was the Fakhri Sextant, an astronomical instrument with a radius of 40m. Ulugh Beg calculated that the stellar year is 365 days, 6 hours, 10 minutes and 8 seconds – just 62 seconds more than modern day estimates!	

Section 1.08 Unit 6B Micro-organisms

Learning Objectives Children should learn:	(i) Examples of possible teaching activities	Reference to curriculum materials
that some micro-organisms can cause common illnesses	This study unit makes strong links between personal and community hygiene and illness. Cleanliness is a familiar concept to Muslim students as general cleanliness is one of the pillars of health in Islam, especially ceremonial washing and performing ablutions several times every day. Muslim students will be familiar with the verse from the Qur'an 'Cleanliness is part of being faithful'.	

Section 1.09 Unit 5B Life cycles

Learning Objectives Children should learn:	(i) Examples of possible teaching activities	Reference to curriculum materials
that adults have young and that these grow into adults which in turn produce young	Muslim students are not forbidden or restricted from receiving sex education. However, the following suggestions might create a more relevant learning environment for Muslim students: ■ It will be the general view amongst Muslims that sex education should start at home with parents and must be considered to be age-appropriate.	

Section 1.09 Unit 5B Life cycles (continued)

Learning Objectives Children should learn:	(i) Examples of possible teaching activities	Reference to curriculum materials
that adults have young and that these grow into adults which in turn produce young	■ Sex is seen as a healthy act, an act of worship, or *ibadah*, if practiced within marriage. Islam takes a balanced view and encourages sex for both pleasure and procreation. ■ Teaching could be customised and adapted to maintain the appropriate *Adab* (etiquette) and to create an Islamic context for learning. For example, the language should not be graphic and books that are used should not contain photographs; diagrams should be enough to teach about the human body. ■ There will be parts of the learning that should take place in single gender groups. It is preferred that teachers are of the same sex as the pupils and preferably married. ■ Personal hygiene (*Taharah*) is an important part of Islamic life, particularly washing in preparation	

Section 1.09 Unit 5B Life cycles (continued)

Learning Objectives Children should learn:	(i) Examples of possible teaching activities	Reference to curriculum materials
	for prayer. This presents a natural and familiar context for learning. For example during discussion about menstruation, the appropriate method of cleaning, in this case *Ghusl*, when a period is over, will be familiar to Muslim girls as they will probably have learned this before the age of 11.	
	■ Consider having someone with a counselling background to speak to Muslim students about the topic, since issues may come up which inexperienced teachers may be unable to handle. For example, if a Muslim student discloses sexual abuse to a teacher after a class or discussion on gender relations, the teacher needs to understand the gravity of this in relation to Islamic belief.	

Section 1.19 Unit 6F How we see things

Learning Objectives Children should learn:	(i) Examples of possible teaching activities	Reference to curriculum materials
that light travels from a source **that we see light sources because light from the source enters our eyes**	Around 1000CE, Ibn Al-Haytham (sometimes known as Alhazen) discovered that light travels in straight lines. He also developed the earlier Greek idea that light reflects off objects and enters the eye, rather than the contemporary belief that light was emitted by the eye.	
that light from an object can be reflected by a mirror	Glass mirrors were in use in Islamic Spain as early as the 11th century. Although it is commonly taught that the Venetians invented mirrors in 1291, it has been shown that they developed earlier work by Syrian artisans almost 200 years earlier.	

Key Stage 3

In their extensive scientific response to the new Key Stage 3 programmes of study the FSTC considered that the revised science programme offered a good opportunity for including many contributions the Muslims made in various scientific fields. They identified the following areas which we reproduce here more or less in their entirety.

1. Energy

There are three areas where the curriculum can expand:

■ Wind and water energy: Windmills and Waterwheels: The programme investigates many types of energy but does not refer to wind and water energy. Pupils should, however, learn about the invention of the windmill and water raising machines.

The windmill was first built in the 7th century in the vast deserts of Arabia and Persia. Early windmills were two-storey buildings built on castle towers, hilltops or their own platforms. Driven horizontally by six or twelve sails, the height of the millstones were adjustable so that grains could vary in size. This was an engineering marvel at the time. They rapidly spread across the world.

The waterwheel, known as *Noria* from Biblical times in the Middle East, still exist at Hama on the river Irontes in Syria, although they are no longer in use. From Syria, the Muslims brought the *Noria* to Spain when it was under their rule and from there it spread into Europe and Britain.

- Light and Ibn Al-Haytham: The programme calls for a practical study of light including reflection and colour perception. It is appropriate to refer to the work of Ibn Al-Haitham (965-1039 CE) and his various discoveries about the nature and behaviour of light including that light travels in straight lines, the path of light can be represented by rays and the laws of the light reflection and refraction.

- Fuel and *Naft*: The current Key Stage 3 science programme provides two sections investigating the nature and character of fuel. This is an opportunity to refer to the characteristics of petrol which were discovered by Muslim chemists.

2. Motion: Al-Jazari machine

The investigation of linear motion and rotation provides an opportunity to refer to the machines of Al-Jazari (13th century, from Diyar Bakir, Turkey), especially the water raising machine where he used a crank which translated rotary motion into linear motion. This was the earliest example of such a system.

3. Chemical reaction, changing state: Distillation

The programme of study refers to distillation. This section can be expanded to describe how the separation process was established by Jabir Ibn Hayyan (722-815CE) and Al-Kindi (801-873), both from Iraq, to obtain alcohol and to make perfume and medical drugs.

4. Body System: Ibn Al-Nafis and Ibn Sina

- The discussion of the circulatory system should refer to the lesser circulation system as discovered by Ibn Al-Nafis (1210 -1288), who was the first to explain how the blood moves between the lungs and the heart. In his treatise '*Commentary on the Anatomy of the Canon of Avicenna*', Ibn Al-Nafis accurately explained the role of the heart and lungs, emphasising that blood was purified in the lungs, when it was refined on contact with the air inhaled from the outer atmosphere.

■ The discussion of the Skeletal System ought to include the work of Ibn Sina (*Avicenna*) on the skeletal system and bone fracture. In his manuscript, famously known as the *Canon*, Ibn Sina did not only describe various bones of the human body but also discussed their disease and fracture and how they could be treated.

5. Drugs: Drug capsules and herbal medicine
The drug section deals with both prescribed and non-prescribed drugs.

■ In prescribed drugs one can refer to how drugs are taken in the form of injections, tablets and capsules. Reference should be made to Al-Zahrawi (936-1013) from Cordoba in Spain, who introduced the first prototype of the capsule drugs by enveloping drugs in a sheep's intestine.

■ The section on non-prescribed drugs should refer to herbal medicine as an historic and contemporary alternative. Muslim pharmacists were skilled in extracting and preparing herbs for medicinal purposes. The spread of herbal medicine and many medical plants into Europe and England was carried through the Muslims.

6. Disease: Ibn Sina
■ In discussion of disease, its history, treatment and prevention, the curriculum should refer to the work of Ibn Sina (980-1037) on his diagnosis and treatment of various diseases. Much of this work is found in the *Canon*, a medical encyclopaedia described as the most famous medical textbook ever written, because it is a unique reference full of all medical knowledge, gathered from many civilisations. It remained in use in medical schools at Louvain and Montpellier until the 17th century, and according to the Journal of UNESCO it was still in use at Brussels University until 1909, well into the age of 'modern medicine'.

■ The second major reference point is the development of hospitals and their role in the treatment and cure of diseases. Muslim hospitals were the forerunners of our modern hospitals as they undertook many of the same functions and had an advanced system of patient admissions.

7. Geological Events

The investigation of sedimentary and metamorphic rocks does not provide any historical account of how various explanations evolved and who was behind them. It is relevant to refer here, too, to the work of Ibn Sina, especially his *Book of Cure,* in which he provided accurate explanations of many geological phenomena such as meteorology. He presented a complete compendium of the knowledge of his day about what happens on the Earth: the formation of mountains and their contribution to the formation of clouds, the sources of water, the origin of earthquakes, the formation of minerals, and the diversity of the earth's terrain. Many of these findings are now ascribed to James Hutton, who lived in England in the 18th century.

8. The story of the solar system

The Key Stage 3 science programme provides an interesting historical background to the evolution of our understanding of the solar system, referring to works of the ancients, the Egyptians and the Greeks but then jumps to Leonardo da Vinci in the 15th century. The huge developments made by Muslim astronomers before them must be included.

These study units have great potential to reflect Muslim experience and heritage and are taken from the *1001 Inventions* teachers pack

Unit 7e	Acids and alkalis
Unit 8k	Light
Unit 7d	Variation and classification
Unit 9k	Speeding up
Unit 9L	Pressure and moments
Unit 9m	Investigating scientific Questions

These study units have considerable potential to reflect Muslim experience, but may need preparatory work to contextualise learning, match appropriate resources, or even rewrite key elements:

Unit 7e	Acids and alkalis
Unit 7f	Simple chemical reactions
Unit 8a	Food and digestion
Unit 8c	Microbes and disease
Unit 8d	Ecological relationships
Unit 8k	Light
Unit 8j	Magnets and electromagnets
Unit 9c	Plants and photosynthesis
Unit 9h	Using chemistry
Unit 9j	Gravity and space
Unit 9m	Investigating scientific questions

Useful Muslim resources for Science
Books and journals

Al-Hassani, S T S (2006) *1001 Inventions: Muslim Heritage in Our World*, London: Foundation for Science and Technology

Ashrif S, (1987) Ethnocentrism and Myopia in Science Teaching. *MCT – Multicultural Teaching* 5.1

Dennick R (1992) *Multicultural and Anti-racist Science Education*. Nottingham: School of Education, University of Nottingham

Ditchfield C (1987) *Better Science: Working for a Multicultural Society*. London: Heinemann

Gill D and Levidov L (1987) *Antiracist Science Teaching*. London: Free Association Books

Mears T (1986) Multicultural Approaches to Science. Gundara, J *et al* (eds), *Racism Diversity and Education*. London: Hodder and Stoughton

Peacock A (1991) *Science in Primary Schools: The Multicultural Dimension*. London: Routledge

Reiss M J (1993) *Science Education in a Pluralist Society*. London: Taylor and Francis

Thorp S *et al* (1994) *Race Equality and Science Teaching*. Hertfordshire: Association for Science Education

■ Geography

There are few study units in the QCA schemes that directly reflect Muslim experience and heritage. Many of the other units however, have enormous potential to be developed. The major issue is that the materials have to be gleaned from a wide range of resources – there is no one obvious source. Although time-consuming, this gleaning is a necessary activity if curriculum materials are to be found or created to reflect Muslim experience and heritage. The new Key Stage 3 programmes of study, however, set the right tone, arguing in '*the importance of geography*' that

> geography explains where people are, how places and landscapes are formed, how people and their environment interact, and how a diverse range of economies, societies and environments are interconnected. It builds upon pupils' own experiences to investigate places at all scales, from the personal to the global

This is a wonderful opportunity given that our Muslim pupils or their parents have come from so many places across the globe! 'Geography inspires pupils to become global citizens by exploring their own place in the world, their values and their responsibilities to other people, to the environment and to the sustainability of the planet' (KS3 Programme of Study).

It has been said that Islam is truly a colour-blind religion that can do much to teach the world about inclusion. Muslims live in most countries across the globe and even predominantly Muslim states are scattered across different continents and regions. Although there is no such thing as a Muslim geographical experience or perspective of the world, there is quite clearly a major opportunity to reflect multiple perspectives within the curriculum, not least Muslim. Within a large proportion of the study units the exemplification and context used by the teacher can relate to countries, cultures and communities that affirm and give credibility to Muslim experience.

Geography encourages cultural understanding and diversity by teaching students to appreciate the differences and similarities between people, places, environments and cultures to inform their understanding of societies and economies. It allows them to realise that people's values and attitudes do condition their views about social, environmental, economic and political issues. It involves such key questions as: Who am I? Where do I come from? Who are our neighbours? What is our story? How has our neighbourhood changed over time? Geographical enquiry involves evaluating evidence and questioning sources. All this should contribute to pupils' overall sense of community cohesion.

Key Stage 3 provides a number of curriculum opportunities to bring the topic of development of maps, particularly of the world and Europe, over the years from various cultures especially those from Muslim heritage. Muslim interest in geography developed early. The expansive Muslim world encompassing Asia, Africa and parts of Europe incorporated a large variety of cultural regions, landscapes, climates and environments. General geographical descriptions of these regions soon became a necessity for the central administration, fiscal system and extension of the postal services. In addition to the works of many explorers who provided detailed geographical descriptions of the old world in medieval times, two leading geographers stand out from the rest. Al-Idris (1099-1166) came from Malaga to settle in Palemo to work for the Norman King Roger II. He produced an atlas for King Roger showing earth as round, and marking the continents of Europe, Africa and Asia. Al-Idris produced a huge silver globe for his Norman patron, to show his findings.

Piri Reis (1465-1554) was another geographer who had great influence on the development of cartography. It was in 1929 that scholars working in Turkey's Topkapi Palace Museum discovered the map he made in 1513, the famous 'Map of America', made only 21 years after Columbus reached the New World. The map of Ali Macar shows a remarkable resemblance to modern satellite maps, and a Muslim map of Syria resembles the modern map of the London underground.

In geography pupils get the opportunity to study people, places and environments in different parts of the world. It can inspire them to think about their own place in the world and their rights and responsibilities to other people. By showing how the level of development in different countries is related to the quality of life, pupils begin to learn the principles of sustainable development; explaining the positive and negative effects of development on the environment and on people. More than in any other subject, pupils begin to develop a world view and understand their role as a global citizen, partly by learning about countries and localities with a range of economic backgrounds and raising consciousness about the way communities work in other countries. In terms of the overarching criteria, geography makes a significant contribution to the concepts of interdependence, status and credibility and presents knowledge as normal, not exotic.

Muslim potential within the QCA scheme of work for geography
Key Stage 1 and 2

This study unit has great potential to directly reflect Muslim experience and heritage:

Unit 10	A village in India

These study units have considerable potential to reflect Muslim experience but may need preparatory work to contextualise learning, match appropriate resources, or even rewrite key elements:

Unit 1	Around our school – local area
Unit 4	Going to the seaside
Unit 5	Where in the world, Barnaby Bear
Unit 7	Weather around the world
Unit 8	Improving the environment
Unit 13	Contrasting UK locality
Unit 14	Investigating rivers
Unit 15	The mountain environment
Unit 16	What's in the news?
Unit 18	Connecting ourselves to the world
Unit 19	How/where do we spend our time
Unit 24	Passport to the world

Key Stage 3

These study units have great potential to directly reflect Muslim experience and heritage:

Unit 1	Making connections
Unit 4	Flood disaster
Unit 16	What is development?
Unit 18	The global fashion industry
Unit 19	Tourism – good or bad?

These study units have considerable potential to reflect Muslim experience and heritage, but may need preparatory work to contextualise learning, match appropriate resources, or even rewrite key elements:

Unit 1	People everywhere
Unit 6	Exploring England
Unit 7	Images of a country
Unit 12	Can the earth cope?
Unit 13	France's changing economy
Unit 14	Comparing countries
Unit 15	Passport to the world

Useful Muslim resources for Geography

Books and journals

Marcovitch L (2001) *In the Eye of a Storm: Life on an Island in Bangladesh*. London: Action Aid

Mangla (1995) *A Study of Change and Development in Mirpur, 'Azad' Jammu Kashmir and Pakistan*. South Yorkshire: DEC ISBN 1 897630 04 2

(2003) *Pakistan – Extended Visit Workbook*. South Yorkshire: DEC

Runnymede Trust (2003) *Complementing Teachers*. London: LETTS Educational

■ 'Contrasting lives and localities'

■ 'What's in the news'

■ 'Why did Bashir Ahmed Abdi die?'

■ 'A Fair Day's Pay'

Websites

Ibrahim M Islamic Relief – Reacting to Poverty. Birmingham: Islamic Relief http://www.islamic-relief.com (August 2007)

Oxfam

Bangladeshi photo activity pack compares Sylhey and Oldham

Theodore, *Cairo – four children and their city* (Oxfam) is a video and photo pack for use with 8 – 12 year olds, showing Cairo from different backgrounds.

O'Flynn, *Gariyan – transport in Pakistan* (Oxfam) is an activity pack for 8 – 13 year olds.

www.oxfam.org.uk (August 2007)

TIDE

The thread of the Nile is an activity photo pack about life in modern Egypt. It raises development issues in Egypt for history and geography at KS2.

www.tidec.org (August 2007)

Web searches for 'Multicultural Birmingham' and 'EMA online' also produce several examples from which to draw

Web search for Development Education Centres

■ Design and Technology

Historically the teaching of Design and Technology has often ignored the contribution of various cultural traditions. However, the subject provides an ideal opportunity to demonstrate that no one culture has the monopoly of achievements in Design and Technology. In this subject pupils begin to re-cognise the different needs of people from a range of cultures and to identify ways in which needs have been and could be met. Pupils learn to design and make products and evaluate how a range of different products work, often generating ideas for designing and making by drawing upon the experiences of other people. By providing a stimulating context for projects and by explor-ing the effects of technology on the development of society and their own lives, pupils can begin to explore how different people have developed solu-tions to meet their needs and some of the values and ethics in relation to the application of design and technology.

The new Key Stage 3 programme of study is clear that there is an ethical dimension to the subject combining, as it does, practical and intellectual skills with an understanding of aesthetic, technical, cultural, health, social, emotional, economic, industrial and environmental issues. Pupils explore how products have been designed and made in the past, how they are cur-rently designed and made and how they may develop in the future. As part of the concept of 'cultural understanding pupils learn how products evolve according to users' and designers' needs, beliefs, ethics and values and how they are influenced by local customs and traditions and available materials.' At both key stages pupils learn the principles of sustainable development – a concept dear to Islamic hearts – and understand something of the positive and negative effects of scientific and technological developments on the environment and on people.

Curriculum opportunities

The QCA scheme of work for design and technology, especially at Key Stages 1 and 2 is strongly skill-based and structured around DMAs (design and making activities). Schools typically follow the scheme of work by adopting the given example e.g. toys or slippers, and use these DMAs as the context in which to develop the pupils' skills. The grid below identifies some of the potential within the QCA projects that already offer major or limited potential to reflect Muslim experience because their context or setting has links with Muslim culture and heritage. There is nothing to prevent schools from choos-ing a completely different set of DMAs to develop design and technology skills that is more relevant to Muslim experience and heritage. There are many examples of innovative teachers capturing Muslim pupils' enthusiasm with projects such a ceramic mosques and decorative wooden *Qur'an* display cases. The strand of food technology possibly provides the most obvious point of reference to Muslim experience.

Muslim potential within the QCA scheme of work for design and technology

Key Stage 1 and 2

These study units have great potential to directly reflect Muslim experience and heritage:

Unit 1c	Eat more fruit and veg.
Unit 3b	Sandwich snacks
Unit 4b	Storybooks
Unit 5a	Musical instruments
Unit 5b	Bread

These study units have considerable potential to reflect Muslim experience and heritage, but may need preparatory work to contextualise learning, match appropriate resources, or even rewrite key elements:

Unit 1d	Homes
Unit 2d	Joseph's coat
Unit 4a	Money containers
Unit 5c	Moving toys
Unit 5d	Biscuits
Unit 6d	Slippers

Key Stage 3

These study units have great potential to directly reflect Muslim experience and heritage:

Unit 7a	Understanding materials
Unit 7b	Designing and making for yourself
Unit 7e	Activity week
Unit 8a	Exploring materials
Unit 8b	Designing for clients
Unit 8e	Producing batches
Unit 8f	World of professional designers
Unit 9c	ICT links to outside world

This study unit has considerable potential to reflect Muslim experience and heritage, but may need preparatory work to contextualise learning, match appropriate resources, or even rewrite key elements:

Unit 7d	Using ICT to control a display

In their submission to the draft QCA programmes of study the Foundation for Science Technology and Civilization identified a plethora of possible connections with Muslim heritage. They suggested that teachers could use the historical development of products like soap, musical instruments, building with environmental features, such as the courtyard houses of Baghdad, Damascus, Fez and Cordova; the development of the automatic machines, such as water, spring and gravity operated clocks, the crank and reciprocal motion, the worm and wheel, the cam shaft and the bevel gear; surgical devices such as forceps, syringes and cat-gut; calculating machines and instruments such as astrolabes, armillary spheres, planetary motion models and Abacus – all of which are excellent examples of the debt the modern world design and technology owes to our Islamic past.

An example of environmental design and sustainability is the Sulaimaniya mosque in Istanbul built by the famous Ottoman Architect Sinan. The smoke from the thousands of oil lamps and candles is guided through aerodynamically driven conduits to a filter room above the main gates to ensure the exterior air remains clean. The filtered soot is then poured into a pond of water to be mixed and treated to produce ink for writing manuscripts.

The origins of fibre reinforced materials, the technology of Damascus steel swords, wood construction of ships, cannons and their arrival in Europe, the world's first gliding flying machine of Abbas Bin Firnas of Spain and the use of light all provide further examples for teachers to incorporate.

Useful Muslim resources for Design and Technology
Books and journals
Brown B (2001) *Combating Discrimination: Persona Dolls in Action.* Stoke on Trent: Trentham

Eggleston J (2001) *Teaching Design and Technology.* Berkshire: Open University Press. Chapter 5 deals with race.

Hall G (1995) *Toys and Games Around the World.* Hove: Wayland

King A *et al* (1993) *The Multicultural Dimension of the National Curriculum.* London: Falmer Press. Chapters by Robinson and Eggleston on Technology

Papanek V (1971) *Design for the Real World: Human Ecology and Social Change.* New York: Pantheon Books

Siraj-Blatchford J (1996) Science, Technology and Anti-racist Education. *Multicultural Teaching* 14.2

Websites
Islam City

Contains information about spectacular Islamic metalwork from the 1300s (Art of the Mamluks www.islamicity.com (August 2007)

Toys Toys Toys Newham LEA have developed some culturally inclusive curriculum projects, including this one for KS1, developed upon the Oxfam video resource 'Toying with technology'.

■ Physical Education and Sport
PE is a skill-based curriculum that is based upon major sports and games. Physical activities *per se* do not provide much of an opportunity to reflect experience, save in the area of Dance where Muslim traditions and experience can provide a rich resource. Islamic tradition and modern practice includes dance forms within worship and at times of celebration. Schools need to be aware of the preference of some Islamic families to use only the voice and untuned percussion to create music. Schools also need to be aware of some of the issues faced by Islamic pupils in PE: e.g. full length swimsuits and single gender sessions for swimming, separate changing even from an early age.

There may also be opportunities, especially in Key Stage 1 and Key Stage 2 where there is less reliance upon major sports, to use minor games and physical activities from other cultures. These can provide great opportunity to develop social skills involving co-operation and collaboration. Learning *about* PE however (as opposed to 'doing' PE), especially in the study of sporting achievement, provides massive potential to reflect upon some of the main Muslim role models in the UK and abroad. Some sports and games in the PE curriculum are strongly linked with certain Islamic countries, e.g. cricket, and provide good opportunities for cultural role models to be given prominence.

Some major sports, notably football at present, are proactive in widening participation from ethnic minorities and stamping out racism. Many schools are using the education packs provided by these sports associations within their PE and Citizenship schemes.

Muslim potential within the QCA scheme of work for PE and sport
Key Stage a and 2
These study units has great potential to directly reflect Muslim experience and heritage:

KS1	Dance (2 units)
KS2	Dance (4 units)

These study units have considerable potential to reflect Muslim experience and heritage, but may need preparatory work to contextualise learning, match appropriate resources, or even rewrite key elements:

KS1	Games activities (2 units)
KS2	Invasion games (4 units)
KS2	Striking and fielding games (2 units)
KS2	Net/wall games (2 units)

Key Stage 3
This study unit has great potential to directly reflect Muslim experience and heritage:

KS3	Dance (4 units)

Useful Muslim resources for PE and sport

Books and journals

Kaminski R (1995) *Children's Traditional Games: Games from 130 Countries and Cultures.* Oxford: Greenwood Press

Orlando L (1999) *The Multicultural Game Book.* London: Scholastic Professional books. Introduces more than 70 traditional games from 30 countries.

Websites

Show Racism the Red Card
www.theRedcard.org (August 2007)

Santhari New Asian Dance Theatre Company supports social, spiritual and aesthetic development through dance and story telling. (5 Alexander Grove, London, N12

■ Religious Education

RE has been extensively reviewed and a national non-statutory framework was produced in 2004 (www.qca.org.uk/qca_7886.aspx). In 2007 the QCA developed their new programmes of study, also non-statutory for Key Stage 3, Key Stage 4 and Years 12 -13. To date, RE syllabuses have been determined by local Standing Advisory Committees for Religious Education (SACREs). Each Local Authority has its own syllabus and these are generally accessible through the web. Too much detail and depth is available to be reproduced here but most materials are available commercially or through the web.

It is in RE that pupils can learn that people in their own community and around the world have different belief systems which have certain things in common. Pupils learn about the moral and social obligations we have towards each other and the importance of social justice to belief systems. Pupils should learn about the world's major religions and about how each individual is important. This should develop an understanding of, and empathy for, other points of view. They should begin to understand the commonalities of quests for spirituality and consider the different influences on individuals and communities. RE also introduces beliefs about the world and how it should be cared for.

RE provides an ideal opportunity to celebrate different national, religious and ethnic identities. As Islam is one of the main 'comparative' religions there is considerable material available to support the relevant study units. Almost every publisher of educational resources for RE has a good range of resources and artefacts for teachers and pupils to reflect Muslim experience. However, care must be taken in the selection of text books and materials from websites, as they may be poorly researched, narrow or insensitive.

Muslim potential within the QCA scheme of work for religious education
Key Stage 1

These study units have considerable potential to reflect Muslim experience, but may need preparatory work to contextualise learning, match appropriate resources, or even rewrite key elements:

Recpn	Who was Noah?
Unit 1a	What does it mean to belong?
Unit 1b	Belonging – in Christianity?
Unit 1c	Christians and gifts at Christmas
Unit 1d	Beliefs and practice – generic
Unit 1e	Jews expressing beliefs in practice
Unit 1f	Visiting a church?
Unit 2c	Celebrations – generic
Unit 2d	Visiting a place of worship – generic

Key Stage 2

These study units have lots of potential to directly reflect Muslim experience:

Unit 5a	The importance of Muhammad
Unit 5b	The beliefs and practices of Muslims
Unit 6b	The role of the mosque
Unit 6d	The importance of the Qur'an

This study unit has considerable potential to reflect Muslim experience, but may need preparatory work to contextualise learning, match appropriate resources, or even rewrite key elements:

Unit 3e	The difference faith makes
Unit 4d	Religions in our neighbourhood
Unit 6a	Worship and community
Unit 6c	The importance of sacred texts
Unit 6f	Expressing faith through the arts

Key Stage 3
This study unit has great potential to directly reflect Muslim experience:

Unit 9a	Rites of passage

These study units have considerable potential to reflect Muslim experience, but may need preparatory work to contextualise learning, match appropriate resources, or even rewrite key elements:

Unit 7a	Where do we look for God?
Unit 7c	Religious figures – generic
Unit 8c	Beliefs and practices – generic
Unit 8e	A visit to a place of worship
Unit 9b	Where did the universe come from?
Unit 9c	Why do we suffer?
Unit 9d	Special places for believers

Useful Muslim resources for Religious Education
Books
Ahsan M M (1979) *The Children's Book of Islam*. London: The Islamic Foundation

Aylett J F (2001) *The Muslim Experience*. London: Hodder Murray

Cole W O (1991) *Moral Issues in Six Religions*. Portsmouth: Heinemann

Hamid A W (1989) *Islam – The Natural Way*. Kent: MELS Publishing
A usable resource for teachers about what Islam is and what it means for each person.

Khan A D (2001) *Muslim Imam: My life, My Religion*. London: Franklin Watts. One of a series of books about religious leaders

Owen R J (1998) *Free at Last: The Story of Martin Luther King*. Norwich: Religious Education Press

Sarwar G (1998) *Islam – Beliefs and Teachings*. London: Muslim Educational Trust

Tames R (1999) *World Religions: Islam*. London: Franklin Watts
Explains main facts and shows how belief affects the lives of Muslims

Wood A (1998) *Homing in: A Practical Resource for Religious Studies in Primary Education*. Stoke on Trent: Trentham books

Websites
Bellingham P (2006) *Religious Education in the Primary Years*. Staffs CC www.sln.org.uk/re (August 2007)

Master Islam
http://www.mastersport.co.uk/education/islam.htm (August 2007)

The Muslim Council of Britain
http://www.mcb.org.uk/ (August 2007)

■ ICT

As a curriculum area, ICT is relatively content free and concerned with a set of generic skills. It is quite a new area of learning so has few connections with the history of Muslims. Modern Muslims, however, are beginning to maximise the opportunities provided by the internet to connect people, ideologies and organisations around the world. One of the major sources of information about the *ummah* is the use of the internet sites, some of which can contribute to the radicalisation of young British Muslims. Internet keyword searches provide a wealth of information to support Islamic studies and especially the historical and scientific tradition within Islam. Islamic supplementary schools, madrasahs and mosque schools here and abroad are beginning to realise the potential of ICT to provide e-resources for their curricula. ICT provides the opportunity to become embedded across the curriculum as a vehicle and environment for learning in many other subjects and the areas with good potential are identified in the grid below.

ICT enables pupils to gather information from a variety of sources and learn to use a wide range of ICT tools and information sources to support their work. Pupils learn how ICT connects local, national and international communities and can lead them to explore the impact of ICT on global interdependence. It can provide opportunities for pupils to exchange and share information, develop pupils' enquiry skills and encourage them to reflect critically on the wider use of ICT in the world outside school. ICT opens up new ways of working that enable pupils to work with others to develop and evaluate their work, and to reflect critically on a range of issues. ICT teaches pupils to use the internet to discuss and debate issues with others and for individual research and information. The internet also provides the opportunity to contact people in other countries who can talk about their own experience of life in a contrasting area, and compare this with their own.

Key Stage 1

These study units have considerable potential to reflect Muslim experience, but may need preparatory work to contextualise learning, match appropriate resources, or even rewrite key elements:

Unit 1b	Using a word bank
Unit 1d	Labelling and classifying
Unit 1e	Pictograms
Unit 2a	Writing stories: Using text

Unit 2b	Creating pictures
Unit 2c	Finding information

Key Stage 2

This study unit has great potential to directly reflect Muslim experience:

Unit 4b	Images in repeated patterns

This study unit has considerable potential to reflect Muslim experience, but may need preparatory work to contextualise learning, match appropriate resources, or even rewrite key elements:

Unit 3a	Combining text and graphics
Unit 3e	E-mail
Unit 4a	Writing for different audiences
Unit 4d	Questionnaires and pie charts
Unit 6a	Multimedia presentation

The new programmes of study at Key Stage 3 and Key Stage 4 outline the importance of ICT in the contemporary world. It is not merely an information tool but 'acts as a powerful force for change in society and citizens should have an understanding of the social, ethical, legal and economic implications of its use'. ICT enables rapid access to ideas and experiences from a wide range of people, communities and cultures, and allows pupils to collaborate and exchange information on a wide scale. 'ICT capability is fundamental to participation and engagement in modern society'. Pupils will explore how ICT changes the way we live, examine its ethical implications and be taught to recognise the issues of risk, safety and responsibility surrounding its use. Crucially, pupils need to be taught that information must not be taken at face value, but must be analysed and evaluated to take account of its purpose, author, currency and context. This includes examining the source of the information to make judgements on its plausibility and accuracy, and to assess bias and partiality.

These study units have considerable potential to reflect Muslim experience, but may need preparatory work to contextualise learning, match appropriate resources, or even rewrite key elements:

Unit 2	Information and presentation
Unit 3	Processing text and images
Unit 8	Public information systems
Unit 9	Publishing on the web
Unit 10	Information – reliability, validity, bias
Unit 14	Global communication

■ Modern Foreign Languages

The original CREAM report concluded that there were few opportunities to reflect the Muslim experience and heritage within the National Curriculum in MFL. Since its publication, however, the educational world has moved on quite dramatically. For some years Muslim students have been able to achieve accreditation in heritage languages such as Turkish, Bengali, Gujarati, Punjabi or Urdu and there have been successful examples of young people achieving very high grades in these subjects, often taught in the complementary/supplementary sector. In addition, learning Arabic has become increasingly popular with young Muslims. Argument has raged for some years over the inclusion of the adjective 'foreign', especially as Britain is multi-lingual and especially as the heritage languages of many of our Muslim pupils are the main means of communication at home. It is now possible to learn heritage languages and Arabic at Key Stages 2, 3 and 4 within mainstream settings.

The revised programme of study at Key Stage 3, for example, makes explicit reference to Arabic and Urdu and allows schools the freedom to choose which languages they teach. It is equally explicit about the importance of languages, 'Languages are part of the cultural richness of our society and the world in which we live and work. Learning languages contributes to mutual under-standing, a sense of global citizenship and personal fulfilment'. The pro-gramme also emphasis the key concept of intercultural understanding where language study helps learners appreciate the richness and diversity of other cultures and offers opportunities to explore identities and become aware of the similarities and the contrast between cultures. It also helps, learners re-cognise that there are different ways of seeing the world, and this in turn helps promote and develop an international outlook. There are many curri-culum opportunities to help British born English speaking Muslim pupils explore something of their rich linguistic, religious and cultural heritage.

The cognitive benefits of being bilingual or multilingual are well researched and the DfES *Languages for All: from Stimulating to Delivering* (2004), the QCA booklet, *Modern Foreign Languages in the Key Stage 4 Curriculum* and the *Languages Ladder at Key Stage 2* encourage the teaching of community (heritage) languages. There are also various Pathfinder projects underway to support and develop initiatives in this area. As *Every Child Matters*, so every language matters. The social and cultural benefits and contribution to identity formation and inter community cohesion are huge.

Faith, however, is the key – and that faith is transmitted through Arabic. As the MCB (2007) succinctly put it:

> Arabic, the language of the Qur'an, holds an important status for all Muslims regardless of their linguistic backgrounds. All Muslim children learn to read and recite the Qur'an in Arabic, and are required to perform their prayers and supplications in this language. Offering Arabic as an option in both primary and secondary schools would provide Muslim children with wider linguistic skills and offer greater access to their religious and cultural heritage, thus giving them a stronger sense of self-esteem and achievement.

■ Mathematics

In mathematics pupils can begin to use number in a range of different contexts and explore number patterns from various cultures. Islamic tradition is rich in the development of geometry and there are also many notable Islamic scholars who made significant discoveries. Pupils can consequently develop an understanding of the universality of mathematics, showing that mathematicians from many cultures have contributed to the development of modern thinking. As they make progress, pupils can apply their mathematical skills to interpreting statistics, analysing and critically assessing what these mean for people's everyday lives. By using maths as a language for communication with young people around the world and providing opportunities for practical data handling and the exchange of data with peers in other countries, mathematics can contribute to contemporary cultural diversity.

The content of mathematics is almost entirely skill-based and the learning objectives within the NNS and Key Stage 3 strategy offer some potential to directly or potentially reflect Muslim experience in the teaching content they describe. However, as with other skill-based frameworks, there is massive potential to set mathematical learning centrally within a context that is relevant to the experience of pupils. Whether it be data handling exercises, numeracy problem solving or open-ended investigations, many areas of maths provide the opportunity to contribute to the ongoing work throughout school that promotes Muslim perspectives.

Teachers need to ensure that they

- portray balanced, positive images that don't reinforce stereotypes or prejudice

- highlight mathematics from other cultures so that Maths isn't seen to have a solely white European history.

Muslim potential within the National Numeracy Strategy
Key Stage 1 and 2

The teaching and learning within these objectives has considerable potential to reflect Muslim experience and heritage, but may need preparatory work to contextualise learning, match appropriate resources, or even rewrite key elements:

Recpn	Counting
Recpn	Reading and writing numbers
Recpn	2D shape
Y1-Y3	Counting, numbers and sequences
Y1-Y3	Properties of 2D and 3D shapes
Y4-Y6	Pencil and paper procedures
Y4-Y6	Properties of 2D and 3D shapes

The teaching and learning within these objectives has limited potential to reflect Muslim experience, but may need preparatory work to contextualise learning, match appropriate resources, or even rewrite key elements:

Recpn	Reasoning about numbers/shapes
Recpn	Problems with 'real life' and money
Recpn	Position, direction and movement
Y1-Y3	Reasoning about numbers and shapes
Y1-Y3	Line symmetry
Y1-Y3	Position and direction
Y1-Y3	Organising and using data
Y4-Y6	Properties of numbers, sequences

Y4-Y6	Reasoning number or shapes
Y4-Y6	Problems involving time
Y4-Y6	Position and direction
Y4-Y6	Angle and rotation
Y4-Y6	Interpreting, organising data
Y4-Y6	Position and direction
Y4-Y6	Organising and using data

Key Stage 3 and 4

The new programmes of study offer considerable potential to include Muslim experience and heritage. The Key Concepts refer to 'recognising the rich historical and cultural roots of mathematics.' As the FSTC put it,

> The history of mathematics gives the Muslims the lion share of influence in developing this science, which began with Al-Khawarizmi's work, when he introduced the beginnings of algebra. It was a revolutionary move away from the Greek concept of mathematics, which was essentially based on geometry. Algebra was a unifying theory that allowed rational numbers, irrational numbers and geometrical magnitudes to be treated as 'algebraic objects'. It gave mathematics a whole new dimension and a development path, much broader in concept than before. The works of Al-Karaji (953-1029), from Baghdad, Iraq and Umar Al-Khayyam (1048-1122), from Nisapur, Iran made much of what we know of today's mathematics

The range and content sections include number and algebra which could be better understood if put in their historical context. So there is a real need for a small section about the history of Algebra, which should include the Muslim contribution. Similarly, the section on statistics would benefit from the inclusion of medieval and Islamic statistical sources. The use of medieval and Islamic coins, weights and data will provide a greater exercise for children to develop their skills in sorting, classifying and comparing measures and values. The inclusion of trigonometrical relationships allows teachers to refer to Al-Battani, Al-Biruni and Al-Khawarizmi, Muslim scholars who first used these expressions. Al-Battani was the first to use the expressions 'sine' and 'cosine', defining them as lengths, rather than the ratios we know them as today. The tangent was referred to by Al-Battani (858-929) as the 'extended shadow', the shadow of a notional horizontal rod mounted on a wall. In the 11th century Al-Biruni (973-1050) defined the trigonometric functions of tangent and cotangents, which were inherited in a tentative form from the Indians. Al-Khwarizmi (780-850) developed the sine, cosine and trigonometric tables, which were later translated to the West. The Arabic word *Geb* for an angle – the ratio of the side facing the angle divided by the hypotenuse – means 'the pocket' which also, in Arabic, means sinus (in an anatomical sense) and this found its way into Latin (sinus) and English (sine).

Within the existing schemes of work, the following teaching and learning objectives have considerable potential to reflect Muslim experience and heritage, but may need preparatory work to contextualise learning, match appropriate resources, or even rewrite key elements:

Y9 ext	Pythagoras' theorem
Y9 ext	Triangle construction/congruence

Key Stage 3

The teaching and learning within these objectives have some potential to reflect Muslim experience, but may need preparatory work to contextualise learning, match appropriate resources, or even rewrite key elements:

Y7	Letters representing variables
Y7	Using probability scale
Y7	Solving word problems
Y8	Column x and / with decimals
Y8	Graphs, charts and ICT
Y8	Algebra geometry graph problems
Y9	Statistical enquiry projects
Y9 ext	Bias in statistics
Y9 ext	Analysing statistical enquiry
Y9 ext	Understanding data limitations

Useful Muslim resources for mathematics
Books
Bailey P and Shan S J (1991) *Multiple Factors: Mathematics for Equality and Justice*. Stoke on Trent: Trentham books

El-Said I and El-Bouri T (1997) *Islamic Art and Architecture – The system of geometric design*. Reading: Garnet Publishing

Krause M (2000) *Multicultural Mathematics Materials*. Illinois: National Council of Teachers

Haskins J (1988-1996) *Count your way series*. Various publishers

Seattle Public Schools Mathematics Office (1984) *Multicultural Mathematics Posters and Activities*. Illinois: National Council of Teachers of Mathematics

Ross A (1984) *The Story of Mathematics*. London: A&C Black

Runneymede Trust (2003) *Complementing Teachers*. London: LETTS Educational

- 'Reasoning and generalising about numbers'
- 'Shape Space and Measures'
- 'Equivalent Fractions'

Websites
Devlin, K (2002) *The Mathematical Legacy of Islam*
www.maa.org/devlin/devlin_0708_02.html (August 2007)

Fought, S (1997) *Mayan Arithmetic*
www.mathforum.org/k12/mayan.math (August 2007)

Historical Connections (AIMS Education Foundation)
http://wwws.aimsedu.org/aims_store/Historical-Connections-in-Mathematics-Vol.-III-p-992.html (August 2007)

Mackenzie, D (2001) *A sine on the road to Mecca*
www.americanscientist.org/template/AssetDetail/assetid/14679 (August 2007)

QCA (2007) *Respect for ALL*
http://www.qca.org.uk/qca_6753.aspx (August 2007)

Symmetry 2000
www.bangor.ac.uk/~mas009/pcont.htm (August 2007)

A web search on 'qibla map projections Mecca' gives an informative article about cartography of medieval Muslims.

■ English

In English, most schools follow the National Literacy Scheme and Key Stage 3 strategy closely, although there are occasions where they supplement, enhance and adapt their planning with other resources and ideas. English affords pupils an ideal opportunity to reflect the wide range of experience, including Muslim, offered through reading about people, places and cultures, in both fiction and non-fiction books.

Finding Muslim experience in accessible literature is not easy. There are authors and poets from which to draw, but they are predominantly from the Asian sub-continent. Much of the material is Asian or Indian in the widest sense and care has to be taken to distinguish the origin of the faith group in order to ensure Muslim perspectives. Authors from Pakistan, Bangladesh, Turkey and other Muslim countries are likely to be Muslim. There is to date little writing available that reflects the British Muslim experience.

The best critical source books are published by NATE. Their *Multicultural literature is the classroom, teachers accounts of innovative work with years five to twelve* (ed. Goody and Thomas) provides some interesting examples of teacher and pupil practice in arrange of settings. The NATEPACK *Multicultural Perspectives in the English Curriculum* edited by Joan Goody on behalf of the committee for Multicultural and Anti-racist Teaching, although published in 1992, is still the best source of materials and inspiration available. Many of the references listed below are taken from NATE publications.

Muslim potential within the National Literacy Strategy
Key Stage 1 and 2 range of resources

The range of resources selected by schools for teaching and learning within these areas of literacy provides great potential to reflect Muslim experience.

Y1	Poetry and stories with familiar, predictable structures and patterned language from a range of cultures
Y2	Traditional stories, stories and poems from other cultures
Y3	Myths, legends, fables, parables
Y3	Oral and performance poetry from different cultures
Y4	Classic and modern poetry, includes poems from different cultures and times
Y5	Traditional stories, myths, legends, fables from a range of cultures

Key Stage 1 and Key Stage 2 range of resources

The range of resources selected by schools for teaching and learning within these areas of literacy provides limited potential to reflect Muslim experience.

Y1	Stories with familiar settings
Y1	Traditional stories and rhymes
Y1	Poems with patterned and predictable structures
Y1	A variety of poems on similar themes
Y2	Stories and a variety of poems with familiar settings
Y2	Extended stories
Y2	Information texts including non chronological reports
Y3	Stories with familiar settings
Y3	Plays
Y3	Traditional stories with related themes
Y4	Historical stories and short novels
Y4	Range of poetry in different forms
Y4	Information texts linked to other curricular areas
Y5	Choral and performance poetry
Y5	Recounts of events, activities, visits
Y5	Instructional texts, rules, recipes, directions, instructions
Y5	Non chronological reports
Y5	Explanations using content from other subjects
Y6	Comparison of work by significant children's authors and poets
Y6	Autobiography and biography, diaries, journals, letters etc
Y6	Journalistic writing
Y6	Non chronological reports
Y6	Non chronological reports linked to other subjects

The new programmes of study at Key Stage 3 and Key Stage 4 strike a clear culturally inclusive note when they say that, 'Literature in English is rich and influential. It reflects the experiences of people from many countries and times and contributes to our sense of cultural identity.' As part of their cultural understanding pupils should gain a sense of the English literary heritage and engage with important texts in it. They should explore how ideas, experiences and values are portrayed in texts from a range of cultures and traditions; and they should understand how English varies locally and globally, and how these variations relate to identity and cultural diversity. Over time pupils should gain an appreciation of the linguistic heritages that contribute to the richness of spoken and written language.

Schools are offered a range of texts from which to choose but it is not prescriptive. 'The choice of texts should be informed by the cultural context of the school and the experiences of the pupils.' The text could, for example, help pupils explore their sense of identity and reflect upon their own values, attitudes and assumptions. Comparing texts helps pupils to explore ideas of cultural excellence and allows them to engage with new ways in which culture develops. Doing so also allows them to explore the culture of their society, the groups in which they participate and questions of local and national identity.

The teaching and learning within these areas of literacy provide great potential to reflect Muslim experience and heritage.

Y7	Vocabulary: Words in different languages
Y8	Reading for meaning: Bias and objectivity, Implied and explicit meaning
Y8	Understanding the author's craft
Y8	Cultural context
Y9	Different cultural contexts
Y5	Persuade, argue, advise – Influence audience
	Counter-argument – Impartial guidance
	Balanced analysis

There are many other areas of literacy teaching and learning in Key Stage 3 that offer limited potential to reflect Muslim experience. These would produce too cumbersome a table to reproduce here. The full CREAM report containing this information is available on the web at www.sdsa.net.

Useful Muslim resources for English
Books

Chatterjee D Fletcher S and Sutton B (1997) *A little bridge.* West Yorkshire: Pennine Pens

Conteh J (2003) *Succeeding in Diversity: Culture, Language and Learning in Primary Classrooms.* Stoke on Trent: Trentham

Dimock E C (1978) *Literatures of India: An Introduction.* Chicago: University of Chicago Press

Dharnaclker V and A K Ramanujan (1998) *Oxford Anthology of Modern Indian Poetry.* USA: Oxford University Press

Goody J and Thomas K (2004) *Multicultural Literature in the Classroom: Account of Innovative Work with Years five to twelve.* Sheffield: National Association for the Teaching of English (available from www.nate.org.uk)

Issa T (2005) *Talking Turkey: The Language, Culture and Identity of Turkish Speaking Children in Britain.* Stoke on Trent: Trentham

Jamal M (1986) *The Penguin Book of Modern Urdu Poetry.* London: Penguin

Matthews D (1995) *Anthology of Urdu Verse in English.* USA: Oxford University Press

Matthews D, Shackle C, and Hussain S (1985) *Urdu Literature.* London: Urdu Markaz

De Souza E (2001) *Nine Indian Women Poets.* USA: Oxford University Press

Warner R (1992) *Bangladesh is my Motherland.* London: Minority Rights Group

Websites

DfES (2007) The Standards Site
www.standards.dfes.gov.uk/literacy/teaching_resources/?nls=fres&root_top_id=914 (August 2007)

International Children's Digital Library (2007)
www.icdlbooks.org (August 2007)

Khayaal Theatre Company provide some contemporary renderings of Sufi classical texts
http://www.khayaal.co.uk/ (August 2007)

Oliver C *My England*
http://www.carelpress.co.uk/dramascripts2.htm (August 2007)

QCA (2007) *Respect for ALL*
http://www.qca.org.uk/qca_6753.aspx (August 2007)

Tara Arts
http://www.tara-arts.com/HTML/aboutus.htm (August 2007)

Manchester Development Education Project
A guide to children's multicultural books
Poems from many cultures
www.dep.org.uk (August 2007)

■ PSHE: Personal Wellbeing, Economic Wellbeing and Financial Capabilities

2007 saw the introduction of four new non-statutory programmes of study, all appearing under the Personal Social and Health Economic Wellbeing banner. The personal wellbeing programmes appear at Key Stage 3 and Key Stage 4. In addition two PSHE non-statutory programmes appear at Key Stage 4 sub-titled, 'Economic Wellbeing and Financial Capability'. All four programmes of study have great potential to directly reflect Muslim experience and heritage.

Personal Wellbeing

The importance of personal wellbeing is fundamental and makes a major contribution to fostering personal development. As pupils explore similarities and differences between people and discuss social and moral dilemmas, they learn to deal with challenges and accommodate diversity in all its forms. This is particularly important for Muslim pupils both in terms of how they deal with people of different and of no faith, and how they deal with the many differences within their own faith groups. The Key Stage 3 programme builds upon the skills identified in the framework for Social and Emotional Aspects of Learning (SEAL) including self-awareness, managing feelings, motivation, empathy and social skills.

Pupils are encouraged to understand that their personal identity will be affected by various factors and that at certain times and in certain places their Muslim identity will be paramount. At other times their cultural, linguistic, racial, familial or other aspects of their multiple identities will come to the fore. This complexity is equally applicable to the development of relationships where pupils will be encouraged to understand that people have multiple roles and responsibilities in society, and that making positive relationships and contributing to groups, teams and communities is important.

Pupils will learn to deal with challenges and accommodate diversity in all its forms. They will be taught to understand that all forms of prejudice and discrimination must be challenged at every level in our lives. When pupils consider their attitudes and behaviour towards diversity, they should identify similarities as well as differences between people. Learning to empathise with others helps pupils accommodate differences in their lives and accept their responsibility to challenge prejudice and discrimination wherever it is encountered.

As part of the *decision making and managing risk key process* pupils should be able to make informed choices and use strategies for resisting unhelpful peer influence and pressure. A key part of personal wellbeing is the exploration and clarification of personal values which can be complex and sometimes conflict with the values of wider society. Pupils should be able to develop relationships and work positively with others by effectively using the social skills of communication, negotiation, assertiveness and collaboration. They should also be able to value differences between people and demonstrate empathy and a willingness to learn about people different from themselves.

PSHE includes learning about drug, alcohol and tobacco use and misuse. The Muslim perspective on the matters will be very helpful in reinforcing key concepts. Great care must be taken when discussing sexual activity as Muslims are prohibited from any sexual intercourse outside marriage, and homosexuality is expressly condemned. Muslims are, however, encouraged to be understanding of homosexuals with the overall aim of returning them to a permitted relationship.

At Key Stage 4 the study of personal wellbeing should include 'the effect of diverse and conflicting values on individuals, families and communities and ways of responding to them'. This could include some of the most high profile issues like forced marriages, attitudes to those of different sexual orientations and issues of cousin marriage. It should also include a study of how the media portrays young people, one issue particularly sensitive to Muslim youths.

The study of personal wellbeing should also include the roles and responsibilities of parents, carers and children's. A very live debate in the Muslim community relates to the respective roles of fathers and mothers. A key curriculum opportunity identified is that pupils should meet and work with people from the wider community in their schools and through external visits. Several LAs have organised very effective twinning arrangements with other schools and authorities.

Economic Wellbeing and Financial Capacity

This new non-statutory programme of study brings together careers education, work related learning, enterprise and financial capability. It particularly supports the fifth outcome of Every Child Matters: 'achieve economic wellbeing'. It is particularly pertinent to Muslims, given the high rate of unemployment amongst 16-24 year old Muslims and the percentage of Muslim women who are economically inactive.

The programme aims to equip students with the knowledge, skills and attitudes to make the most of changing opportunities in learning and work.

With expanding markets in Arab and other Muslim countries, what are the possibilities for economic development? Students learn to be enterprising, to understand a business environment and the functions and uses of money. They are also taught about the social and moral dilemmas concerning the use of money. These could include how the choices they make as consumers affect other people's economies and environments. It could also cover issues surrounding the Islamic view of interest, Islamic banking and ethical banking.

■ The Foundation Stage

Much of the Foundation Stage curriculum and its early learning goals have the potential to reflect Muslim experience. Many resources are available which can be fed into the curriculum as a matter of course. The excellent work of the Early Years Equality (EYE) organisation provides much of the theoretical and resources-based materials. A visit to their website is essential.

The curriculum guidance in the foundation stage directly refers to ethnicity, culture, religion, home language, mutual respect, celebrating and acknowledging differences and positive resources. Unlike other later curriculum areas much of it can also directly address the experience of Muslim girls. Unusually, there appears to be more Muslim material than African-Caribbean.

Potential within the Foundation Stage

The teaching and learning within these Early Learning Goals have great potential to directly reflect Muslim experience:

Have a developing respect for their own cultures and beliefs and those of other people

Understand that people have different needs, views, cultures and beliefs, that need to be treated with respect

Understand that they can expect others to treat their needs, views, cultures and beliefs with respect

Listen with enjoyment, and respond to stories, songs and other music, rhymes and poems and make up their own stories, songs, rhymes and poems

Use language to imagine and recreate roles and experiences

Retell narratives in the correct sequence, drawing on language patterns of stories

Find out about past and present events in their own lives, and in those of their families and other people they know

---

Begin to know about their own cultures and beliefs and those of other people

Explore colour, texture, shape, form and space in two or three dimensions

Recognise and explore how sounds can be changed, sing simple songs from memory, recognise repeated sounds and sound patterns and match movements to music

Use their imagination in art and design, dance, imaginative and role play and stories music

Express and communicate their ideas, thoughts and feelings by using a widening range of materials, suitable tools, imaginative and role play, movement, designing and making, and a variety of songs and musical instruments

The teaching and learning within these Early Learning Goals has considerable potential to reflect Muslim experience, but may need preparatory work to contextualise learning, match appropriate resources, or even rewrite key elements:

Respond to significant experiences, showing a range of feelings when appropriate

Have a developing awareness of their own needs, views and feelings and be sensitive to the needs, views and feelings of others

Enjoy listening to and using spoken and written language, and readily turn to it in their play and learning

Use talk to organise, sequence and clarify thinking, ideas, feelings and events

Say and use number names in order in familiar contexts

Count reliably up to 10 everyday objects

In practical activities and discussion begin to use the vocabulary involved in adding and subtracting

Talk about, recognise and recreate simple patterns

Observe, find out about and identify features in the place they live and the natural world

Find out about their environment and talk about those features they like and dislike

Recognise the importance of keeping healthy and those things which contribute to this

Useful Muslim resources for the Foundation Stage

Books

Benjamin F (1996) *Skip Across the Ocean.* London: Frances Lincoln Publisher

Haskins J (1988-1996) *Count Your Way series.* Various publishers

EYE
2nd Floor St John's House
St Johns Square
Wolverhampton WV2 4BH
eye@earlyyearsequality.org

Websites

Itchyka – Dana (Man) Asian nursery rhymes http://www.dep.org.uk/bookshop/earlyyears/index.php (August 2007)

Manchester Development Education Project *Early Years – Laying the foundations for race equality* www.dep.org.uk (August 2007)

Portsmouth Ethnic Minority Achievement Team http://www.blss.portsmouth.sch.uk/ (August 2007)

General resources for Muslim issues in education
Books
Aslan R (2005) *No God but God: The Origins, Evolution and Future of Islam*. London: Heinemann

Bewley A (1998) *Glossary of Islamic Terms*. London: Ta-Ha Publishers

Bloom J and Blair S (2001) *Islam: Empire of Faith*. London: BBC

Clark M (2003) *Islam for Dummies*. Indiana: Wiley Publishing Inc

Haw K (1998) *Educating Muslim Girls*. Berkshire: Open University Press

Hewer C T R (2002) *The Essence of Islam*. Hampshire: Alphonsus House

Hewer C T R (2006) *Understanding Islam: The First Ten Steps*. London: SCM Press

Mawdudi S A A (2001) *The Islamic Way of Life*. London: The Islamic Foundation

McDermot M Y and Ashan M M (1980) *The Muslim Guide*. London: The Islamic Foundation

Parker-Jenkins M (1995) *Children of Islam*. Stoke on Trent: Trentham Books

Shain F (2003) *The Schooling and Identity of Asian Girls*. Stoke on Trent: Trentham Books

Sultan S (2004) *The Koran for Dummies*. Indiana: Wiley Publishing

TIDE (2003) *Citizenship and Muslim Perspective – Teachers Sharing Ideas*. Birmingham: TIDE and Islamic Relief

The Runnymede Trust (1997) *Islamaphobia – A Challenge for Us All*. London: The Runneymede Trust

van Dijk L and van Driel B (2007) *Challenging Homophobia*. Stoke on Trent: Trentham Books

Wrigley T (2000) *The power to learn*. Stoke on Trent: Trentham Books

Websites
BBC Religion and Ethics www.bbc.co.uk/religion (August 2007)

F.A.I.R. www.fairuk.org (August 2007)

Frontline: Muslims
http://www.pbs.org/wgbh/pages/frontline/shows/muslims (August 2007)

Global Virtual Classroom
www.virtualclassroom.org (August 2007)

Guardian Documentaries
www.guardian.co.uk/muslimvoices (August 2007)

Islam City
www.islamicity.com/education (August 2007)

Islamic Foundation
www.Islamic-foundation.com (August 2007)

Islamic Relief
www.islamic-relief.com (August 2007)

Islamic Society or Britain
www.isb.org.uk (August 2007)

Muslim Council of Britain
www.mcb.org.uk (August 2007)

Muslim Heritage
www.muslimheritage.com (August 2007)

Teachers TV
http://www.teachers.tv/node (August 2007)

Promoting Cultural Diversity through Islam Oldham School Development Service pack for KS1 and KS2

3

Islamic Arts in the Curriculum

Robert Bunting

Introduction

This chapter is written for everyone concerned with the education of Muslim pupils in the UK. For teachers and school managers it provides information about the arts in Islam, and suggestions for the curriculum. For the benefit of parents and community leaders, it explains aspects of the current practice and philosophy of UK arts education. My own background – that of a non-Muslim music teacher and adviser – will no doubt show through, but I have tried to give a balanced view of all the arts including literature and story-telling.

The chapter starts with an exploration of the various Islamic arts traditions: covering dance, drama, music, poetry, story-telling and visual arts. It then discusses some of the controversies surrounding the arts within Islamic thought, and suggests how UK arts educators might best respond. This leads to some suggested strategies for developing practice in schools, and guidance for teachers, ending with a list of useful resources.

The heart of the chapter lies in the case studies: snapshots of real-life recent activity in a wide range of schools – Infant, Junior and Secondary – including faith schools and a special school. These provide models for teaching, learning and curriculum planning. Many of the snapshots portray children working with Muslim artists – which is indeed an important dimension. But some describe the work of non-Muslim classroom teachers who, drawing purely on their own resources and skills, have taken the time to learn about Islam and the arts.

Young people from Muslim families in the present day UK are wrestling with particularly difficult challenges. They cannot identify completely with the culture of their parents, which may be closely tied to their ethnic group and country of origin. While often building on this, young Muslims inevitably seek to go beyond it. They are naturally influenced by Western youth and popular culture, see themselves as Westerners, but remain wary of some of its aspects. Increasingly they seek their identity in what they see as a purer form of Islam, detached from particular regions or ethnic groups.

These shifts have several important consequences:

- young people tend to reject those aspects of their parents' cultures which they see as un-Islamic

- they seek to adapt Western cultural forms so as to convey Islamic messages

- they are beginning to explore aspects of the world-wide Islamic tradition beyond their own regional or ethnic inheritance

There is therefore a move towards a globalised, 'pure' Muslim culture, taking elements from many different sources. And there is thus great scope for integration between Western and Muslim cultures, for a two-way process of dialogue and change. Already many young Muslim artists are mapping out new artistic territory with remarkable creativity.

> The Birmingham artist Mohamed Ali has linked the age-old Islamic tradition of calligraphy with the contemporary development of graffiti as an art-form; he creates dramatic visual images that use the idiom of the street to reflect on spiritual and social themes, describing his work as 'aerosoul arabic'.

> Cardiff-born musician Sami Yusuf studied at the Royal Academy of Music. He fuses Western classical and popular idioms with rap, Qur'anic chanting, *nasheed* and qawwali idioms and influences from Pakistani, Egyptian and Turkish music, to create powerful songs, again focusing on spiritual and social themes.

> The hip-hop band Outlandish consists of two Muslims – one from Morocco, the other from Pakistan – and a Honduran Catholic. They are based in Denmark, but reach a world-wide audience with songs about the social issues that concern them as Muslims in the West. Their main language is English but they also perform in Urdu, Arabic, Spanish and Danish.

Islamic Arts Traditions

My aim is to provide UK teachers of the arts with information about the rich inheritance of arts traditions in Islam, and to explain how these traditions are developing in the present day. It is the start of a fascinating personal journey: to become aware of the wonderful achievements of Muslim artists of the past, such as the poet Rumi, musician Nusrat Fateh Ali Khan, or the Islamic calligraphers; to make contact with practising artists in our own locality; and to tune in to the exciting contemporary Islamic arts scene both nationally and globally.

You will notice that the main focus in this chapter is on arts activities with a devotional, spiritual or moral purpose. These are the areas where the arts diverge most clearly from their ethnic regional roots. They are also the areas most likely to win the interest and respect of young people who are strongly focused on their faith – what it means to be a Muslim in the West.

But alongside this we must always bear in mind the rich secular cultural elements within the Islamic tradition (which indeed often have a spiritual or philosophical foundation). There are many fine artists in every form who are Muslim but do not focus on religious or devotional elements; to name but a few, singer Natasha Atlas, writer Monica Ali, dancer Sonia Sabri, painter Sajida Asif, all of whom are based in the UK.

Some examples of the better-known Islamic arts traditions are shown in the table below.

	devotional/spiritual/moral	secular/cultural
Music	*Nasheeds* (UK and worldwide), *qawwali* (North India and Pakistan), devotional and morally engaged rap and R'n'B (USA)	*Andalous* music, music of West Africa, Middle Eastern and North Indian classical music, Algerian Rai, European and Indian 'fusion', many folk and popular traditions
Dance	*hadrah* and *sima* – circle and whirling dances of the Sufi dervish sects	Dancing for community celebrations such as weddings or harvest. Contemporary dance groups
Drama	Iraqi and Iranian Shi'ah Ta'ziyah (Ashura) passion plays	Indonesian shadow plays, North Indian village plays, Turkish Karagoz puppets. Contemporary theatre and drama initiatives
Story telling	Sufi tales, Kalilah and Dimnah stories, Mullah Nasruddin (Hoja) stories	Arabian Nights, street entertainers across the Islamic world

	devotional/spiritual/moral	secular/cultural
Literature	Rumi, Hafiz, Attar, the Qasidah Burdah	A vast range of fiction and poetry old and new
Visual arts	Calligraphy, mosque art and architecture, ceramics, textiles	Turkish, Persian and Indian miniatures; Ottoman and Moghul art forms. A vast range of contemporary artists

As we scan this table we can see the outlines of an emerging global Islamic culture, binding Muslim traditions that range from West Africa to Indonesia into one great corpus that informs the work of artists in contemporary Europe and America.

For some educated Muslims this is already a living reality – as even a glance at the Islamic lifestyle magazine Emel (www.emel.com) will show.

But the paradox is that most children of Muslim families and their parents are not at all familiar with Islamic arts traditions from beyond their own ethnic culture. For instance, a Muslim from a Pakistani background may not even have heard of Youssou N'Dour. A key part of the challenge for arts teachers therefore is to introduce young Muslims, as they move beyond the cultures of their parents and of the Western mass media, to their own inheritance.

> Over three lessons, a Year 5 class, most of whom are Muslim, study a colour photograph of a section of wall decoration from the Alhambra Palace in Granada. The image contains three bands of design: the Shahadah in Arabic calligraphy at the top, a geometric pattern of interlaced lines in the middle, and an abstract design based on star shapes of different sizes at the bottom.
>
> They work with their teacher, discussing how lines and dots of different sizes can be translated into musical sounds. They then divide into specialist groups; each group has the task of creating a musical version of one of the bands in the design.
>
> Next, mixed groups are formed, each containing members of all three specialist groups. The new groups have the task of combining their ideas to create a musical interpretation of the whole design.
>
> During this sequence of lessons children are shown photographs of the Alhambra, and the teacher explains that it was built by Muslim rulers in Spain, at a time when Christians, Muslims and Jews lived together peacefully and achieved great things in science and the arts. For homework they carry out further research on the Alhambra and Andalusia.

Before we look at some of the arts in more detail, three general points need to be made.

First and foremost, Islam is a religion of the Word, and literature is the dominant art form. In particular, the spoken word is greatly valued, for instance, the Qur'an is shared through recitation, not silent reading. Story-telling is a high art; the poems of Rumi are often recited to instrumental accompaniment; in popular music rapping is an important element. Music is in fact seen as an adjunct of poetry, with great emphasis on the meaning and literary quality of the lyrics. In the visual arts, text is often an important element, and many artists are inspired by calligraphy, the art of beautiful writing.

Secondly, when we move from an ethnic to an Islamic view of culture, Middle Eastern elements become more important than they are for most of us at present. In poetry for instance, Rumi, Attar, Hafiz and the *Qasidah Burdah* are known and loved by educated Muslims of all ethnic origins.

Thirdly, we have to acknowledge and understand the power of Sufism throughout Islam. This mystical tradition, setting great store by poetry, music and dance, is a vital influence on the work of many Muslim artists. What Sufis seek is nearness to God through ecstasy and trance, and they are prone to describe it in passionate metaphors, even metaphors of drunkenness and desire.

Sufis seek the unifying forces behind all religions – they are proudly inter-faith, welcoming Christian, Jew, Sikh and Hindu as followers of the *Tariqa* or *Path*. And their love of the arts strikes a chord in our art-saturated Western world. Sufism thus has the potential to be a great force for good in the West, bringing Muslim and non-Muslim together.

But for obvious reasons Sufism is somewhat suspect to more orthodox Muslims – there may be respect, but it is wary respect!

■ Poetry

Islamic poetry is a living art form; for instance, a favourite entertainment in Iran today is the *musha'arah*, in which friends gather for the evening to share their favourite poetry. But Islam has kept a special reverence for the work of certain ancient writers, who are known and loved through the Muslim world.

Rumi, who lived and wrote in 13th century Anatolia, is one of the best-selling poets in the world today. A hugely influential Sufi teacher – it was he who established the tradition of the whirling dervishes – he produced a body of poems that combines deep spiritual insight with an earthy humour rather in the spirit of Chaucer.

Hafiz, an Iranian Sufi poet dating from the 14th century, was a master of the ghazal, a poetic form taken up by Indian writers and nowadays often associated with song. His subtle and passionate poems describe spiritual longing through images of flowing tresses and brimming wine cups.

One of the great Islamic poems, a song of gratitude to Allah still recited regularly all over the Muslim world, is *Qasidah Burdah*, The Song of the Cloak, written by Imam Busayri in 7th century Egypt.

The Conference of the Birds by Attar (Iran, 12th Century) is another mystical description of the Sufi tariqah or path to unity with God, described allegorically through the adventures of a flock of birds.

■ Drama

There is very little drama in Islamic tradition, beyond a few folk traditions specific to certain regions and cultural groups, often involving puppetry or shadow plays. In the Iranian and Iraqi *Shiah* traditions, the *Ta'ziyah* passion plays re-enact the martyrdom of Husayn on *Ashura* in the month of *Muharram*.

However, modern artists are developing new forms of drama to meet contemporary needs. For example, Khayaal Theatre Group, based in Luton, creates powerful and colourful theatre using Western drama techniques to explore material from the Muslim tradition, such as the poetry of Rumi, and addresses moral and social issues that concern present-day Muslims.

> A Year 6 class of children from many faith backgrounds, studies stories from Rumi, the renowned poet and Sufi teacher, working with Luqman Ali of Khayaal Theatre Company. The children discuss themes of bullying and courage, then use drama techniques to retell the stories, finding parallel situations in their own lives, centred on the playground or the street.

■ Story telling

This has always appeared to me an accessible performing art that is potentially rewarding and may deserve a higher profile in schools. It is a living tradition in Islam – anyone travelling in the Middle East soon becomes aware of the popularity of story-tellers, who perform in the street or market to admiring crowds.

We all know of the Thousand and One Nights, a distinctly secular collection of stories; more characteristically Islamic are the Bidpai stories, also known as Kalilah and Dimnah stories, animal fables with a strong moral content, rather like Aesop's Fables.

There is also a wonderful corpus of comic stories concerning Mullah Nasruddin, known as Hoja in Turkey, beneath whose paradoxes and cunning simplicity lurks a subtle Sufi sensibility. These can be traced to the 13th century, but are still circulating on many websites today.

> Year 2 children in a school with children from many faith backgrounds work with Asian writer and story-teller Debjani Chatterjee. They learn the Qur'anic story of Shah Sulayman, who could speak the languages of birds and animals, and his love for Bilqis, Queen of Sheba, to whom he sent the Hoopoe as messenger. They look at pictures of Islamic royal palaces such as the Taj Mahaal, and of the magnificent Hoopoe bird. They learn words of greeting in Arabic and Punjabi, and talk about the meaning of the phrase '*al-Salamu'alaykum*'. They act out the story in words and movement, using alliteration to write single lines of dialogue.

> Another Year 2 class in the same school carries out a similar project with writer Simon Fletcher, based on a comical story from the legendary Sufi teacher Mullah Nasruddin, about a trickster stealing a donkey. They retell the story using drama techniques such as hot-seating and freeze-frame.

> In another school, a class of Year 3 children, all Muslim, work with their teacher, re-telling the story of the Lion and the Hare. This is taken from the collection known as Kalilah and Dymna or Bidpai stories, known throughout the Muslim world. They use musical instruments to create a sound-track for the story, expressing the different moods and characters. Since the story is set in the countryside around Baghdad, they study landscape photographs of the area and talk briefly about its history.

■ Visual Arts

Most of the world's visual arts traditions are representational – they create pictures or sculptures that portray the objects, creatures, people we see in the world around us. Some Muslim art also is representational, as for instance Persian and Moghul miniature paintings. But the special gift of Islam to the world is in abstract geometric patterning. This often uses motifs such as sun, stars, and plant forms. It shows itself in architecture, and in tiling, carving and textiles, even in garden design. Combining all these traits, the Alhambra Palace in Granada is one of the world's great artistic masterpieces.

Another characteristic Islamic tradition is in calligraphy – beautiful writing taken a step further so that letters and words become abstract or figurative designs. One common example is to write the *Bismillah*, the opening words of the Qur'an, in the form of a bird.

There is a thriving community of present-day Muslim visual artists, who build on these traditions, often using current technology; many also use collage and other figurative techniques to explore contemporary political and social themes.

> Year 4 children, nearly all of whom are Muslim, work with Muslim artist Shaheen Ahmed. She shows them examples of the tradition of calligraphy, creating beautiful abstract designs from Arabic letter shapes, including some of her own work. The children copy the shapes of single letters, then use inversion, reversal and change of size to make abstract designs out of these shapes. The designs are then used to make prints using a range of colours.

> Next the children are introduced to a software package that can carry out the same procedures. With this they make new designs, using letters from an Arabic font and adding brilliant colour effects.

■ Music

Muslims are called to prayer by the chanting of the *adhan*; they listen to the Qur'an recited in a singing voice with the most beautiful control of pitch and rhythm. Other than this, music plays no part in worship. However, Qur'anic recitation is a highly developed art form in its own right, in which several different styles are recognised, and a particular ornate form is used for public competitive presentations known as *qira'ah*.

There is however a body of popular devotional song under the title of *nasheeds*, or Na'ts in Urdu. The tradition goes back to the earliest days of Islam, when Muhammad (PBUH) was welcomed to Medinah by children singing a song every Muslim still knows, '*Tala'al-Badru 'Alayna*'. It developed through the songs of pilgrims journeying to Mecca and other shrines, almost as a form of folk music, yet is now blossoming into a world-wide industry of recording and performance. *Nasheeds* are usually simple and melodious, but full of eloquence and powerful emotion. Often they use only voices and percussion, but increasingly artists are experimenting with a broader range of sounds and styles. In the USA, *nasheed* groups such as *786* embrace hiphop, rap and R'n'B.

Nasheeds are almost always sung by groups of young men. They are extremely popular with both boys and girls. There is an element of hero worship, which naturally arouses anxiety among older and more conservative Muslims. In fact the group *786* were recently prevented from appearing at a UK venue because in spite of their manifestly devout approach it was felt that their presence might stir up excessive excitement among their teenage girl followers!

The UK boasts some of the most respected performers world-wide, including the Birmingham-based groups Shaam and Aa'siq al-Rasul. Solo artists include

Yusuf Islam and Cardiff-born Sami Yusuf, whose beautiful music extends the possibilities of the *nasheed* to their furthest extent so far.

The Pakistani Sufi tradition gave birth to *qawwali* music. '*Qawal*' means 'to speak or recite', and classic poetry in both Urdu and Farsi is an important element. The music is usually performed by a '*qawwali* party', a group of singers supported by harmonium and percussion players. At root it is an earthy popular music style, with strong melodies and driving rhythm, but *qawwali* is enriched by brilliant virtuoso improvisation from the lead vocalist, which lifts performers and audience alike into a passionate spiritual trance. The late Nusrat Fateh Ali Khan is still revered by musicians of every background world-wide. Abida Parveen is less well-known internationally, but her singing has a spiritual depth that captures the yearning intensity of all Islamic music.

The Sufi spirit can also be heard in the music of Youssou N'Dour of Senegal, particularly in his fascinating album 'Egypt', and that of the ambient trance DJ and devotee of traditional Turkish music, Mercan Dede. Both of these artists use a full range of instruments and all the resources of modern technology.

> Year 8 girls in a secondary Muslim faith school work with Ruth Roberts, Head of Vocal Studies for Birmingham Music Service. They listen to two recordings of the traditional song '*Tala'al-Badru Alayna*'. Although both versions have been arranged by Yusuf Islam, they are very different in mood – one calm and mystical, the other powerful and dramatic. They sing the song, then use a writing frame to make notes about the two recordings, explaining how they differ and how both versions relate to the message and origins of the song.

■ Dance

The case of dance in Islam illustrates the tensions between ethnic culture and faith culture.

Although many Muslims have serious reservations about the acceptability of dance, every country where Islam has a presence preserves its own traditional dances, often associated with times of communal celebration such as weddings or harvest. These are usually condoned by religious leaders, provided men and women never dance together.

The communities of the *diaspora* preserve these dances, but seek to modernise or Westernise them. So, at a traditional Pakistani wedding in the UK there will be '*dhol* nights' of drumming and singing, and dancing sessions where, more and more frequently men and women dance together.

But for many young British Muslims, their faith is what matters, not their parents' beliefs or Western culture. The websites to which they turn for discussion and advice reveal deep unease within the new, more Islamically conscious generation at the rituals of a traditional Pakistani wedding. Surely, dance and music are un-Islamic – above all, men and women should not be dancing together. One young Muslim even told me that if there was to be dancing at her sister's wedding she would not attend.

There is no equivalent of ballet in Islamic countries, but there are many initiatives in contemporary dance. These usually reference culture rather than faith, and to escape suspicion may use some such label as 'expressive movement'. To give one example:

> American dance artist Nicholas Rowe works with El Funoun Popular Dance troupe in Palestine, running dance classes for young people. He is eloquent on the contrast between the proud free movement his students display in class, and the submissive bowed postures they adopt at check-points and when stopped by the security forces.

Islam does have one deep-rooted dance tradition, associated with the Sufi practice of *dhikr*, remembrance of Allah. In the *sima*, participants move round together in a circle with bowing movements. In *hadra*, individuals rotate on the spot, one hand raised to heaven to receive divine energy, the other hand turned downwards to transmit it to the earth. This is the dance familiarly known as that of the whirling dervishes; it is in danger of being trivialised as a tourist attraction, but modern Muslim artists such as musician Mercan Dede are developing it in new contexts which respect its devotional purpose.

> Over four sessions, Year 6 children work with Muslim musician Amran Ellahi of A'asiq al-Rasul and Dervish Arts, who is qualified to teach Sufi movement and music. First he shows them film of the congregation of a Syrian mosque performing a circling dance, *sima*, bowing and chanting rhythmically. Although the children are all Muslims, they are astonished and excited – 'I've never seen anything like that before'. The children learn to do the dance, holding hands and moving round in a circle. They then learn a chant, *dhikr*, using some of the names of Allah to accompany the dance.
>
> Next they study film of the whirling dance of the Turkish dervishes, *hadra*. They practice carrying out the whirling movement. The teacher shows them how the drummers create patterns using two basic sounds, 'dum' and 'tak'. They work in groups inventing similar patterns to accompany the whirling dance.

During the sessions the children have also worked with Yasmin Akhtar of Dervish Arts, exploring the symbolic meaning of the circle – 'it has no beginning and no end' -, and talking about cyclical processes in life such as the seasons, the earth going round the sun and so on. For homework the children write poems on the theme of circles.

At the same time Dervish Arts have been carrying out a simpler version of the project in a special school, working with children with severe autism. Here the addition of dervish costume (long-skirted cloak and conical hat) decorated with motifs of sun and moon has transmitted the messages of the project and has powerful visual impact.

Controversies about the arts within Islam

Over the centuries some Muslims have seen the arts as a threat. In this Islam is no different from Christianity and Judaism. 17th century English Puritans for instance whitewashed over the beautiful paintings on church walls, destroyed stained glass and forbade the use of musical instruments in worship. The difference is that in Islam these attitudes are wide-spread today. Arts educators therefore need to understand something of the range of attitudes to the arts in the various schools of Islamic thought. Real tensions exist, intellectual battles are being fought.

Although all the arts have their controversies, the disputes rage with greatest intensity around music. Here for instance is a selection of comments on music made by distinguished scholars at a conference in London in 1996, taken from Proceedings of the Conference on Islam and Music, Much Ado About Music (Education Society of the Association of Muslim Researchers, 1996).

> Suhaib Hasan: 'Islam tries to create a very pure society. In that pure society, there is no room for any dilly-dallying, for this rocking and rolling, for music at all ... To be a Muslim a person has to relinquish many things. Music is one such renunciation.'

> Ibrahim Hewitt: 'Music per se can be intoxicating, and ... produce trance-like states within listeners ... No longer to be in control of one's senses is de facto to be intoxicated – one way in which Satan distracts people from the remembrance of Allah.'

> Abd al-Rahman Johansen: 'undoubtedly there are pieces of music which inspire a heightened awareness of God's majesty and beauty. Also unquestionably, there is music which appeals directly and solely to the baser ego... Every individual must use their God-given discernment to arrive at an honest decision.'

> Abd al-Lateef Whiteman: 'If the culture is bad, it is more than likely that the music will be so, and conversely good music will spring forth from a good culture. Which

is why we have to refine culture by choosing between good and bad music. Not between music and no music at all.'

Abd al-Lateef Whiteman: 'The barrier against Islam in this society [the UK] is deep. Music is one way that the seeker can by-pass the ... intellectual prejudice against Islam which this society ... continues to propagate ... We should learn how to use music to our advantage'.

All these comments are about music. Yet the range of Islamic attitudes they encapsulate applies equally to the other arts.

These are not just scholarly debates; they show through in the attitudes of ordinary Muslims, and of parents, governors and community leaders in many schools. For each of the arts there is a range of views within Islam, with some aspects distinctly controversial. While most Muslims cautiously accept the arts, within clearly defined limits, there are those who would advocate a complete embargo; some on the other hand would happily allow the arts a wide scope.

In an inner-city primary school with a largely Muslim intake, governors connected with the nearby mosque leadership demand that music, dance and figurative arts be excluded from the curriculum. They are supported by some Muslim members of the teaching staff. The Head teacher insists that the school provide a full arts curriculum, including visiting artists and instrumental music teachers. She is put under extreme pressure, but gradually finds more and more parents supporting her. Changes in the mosque leadership and on the governing body eventually remove the tension, and the school is now able to provide its pupils with a rich artistic education.

■ Visual Arts

Here the area of controversy surrounds portrayals of living things. To create a copy of a lion, a horse, even more a human being, is in a sense to mimic God. One of the sayings of the Prophet, the *ahadith*, makes a particular point of condemning sculpture – indeed, making statues and pictures is one of the major sins of Islam. A milder version of this prohibition would merely avoid portraying the human face. The role of photography is unclear – is it merely a factual record, for journalistic or educational purposes say, or is it an art form and therefore subject to the same restrictions as painting?

There are, in fact, schools of art within Islam that freely portray both animals and people – the Turkish, Persian and North Indian schools of miniature painting for example. Nonetheless, many artists have worked creatively within the orthodox restrictions, creating abstract patterning from plant forms and geometric or letter shapes.

■ Drama

A similar concern to avoid mimicking God suggests that it is wrong to act the part of another human being. One creative solution has been the development of puppetry and shadow plays. In the *Ta'ziyeh* passion plays of the Iranian *Shia* tradition, the text is read from scripts, creating a protective distance between actor and character.

Radio is an important medium, since the actors are not seen and are reading from scripts; in line with key Islamic values, the emphasis is almost entirely on the spoken word. In contemporary Pakistan, radio drama is a valuable tool for transmitting social messages about issues such as child-care and women's health.

■ Music

Again, Islam has a glorious musical tradition, but as we have seen, a significant school of thought is fiercely opposed to the art. This is essentially because music is seen as 'sensuous', associated with loose living, self-indulgence and immorality. The use of the voice may be acceptable, provided the words being sung are devotional or have a moral purpose. But for many the only acceptable accompaniment is a simple drum – all pitched instruments are forbidden.

One way of resolving this issue may be through the use of ICT – for instance, although it may be forbidden to play the clarinet, it might be acceptable to use a clarinet MIDI voice on the computer. Purist thinkers might deny this, insisting that any use of pitched sound is automatically *haram*. But the original *hadith* associates the ban on pitched instruments with specific activities such as dancing and drinking alcohol, so many Muslims would accept the creation of pitched sound using music technology as long as it was in an appropriate venue and context.

■ Dance

If music is sensuous, how much more so dance! For many Muslims dance is nothing more or less than a public expression of sexuality, therefore deeply offensive. To such people, dance is epitomised by belly-dancing, which is seen as pornographic and degrading of women.

More moderate views would recognise the value of folk dance, and even of creative dance for children before puberty, but would insist on the sexes dancing separately. The following extract from the Muslim Council of Britain's guidance to schools on adapting the curriculum to the needs of Muslim pupils puts this point of view clearly:

> Muslims consider that most dance activities, as practised in the curriculum, are not consistent with the Islamic requirements for modesty, as they may involve sexual connotations and messages when performed within mixed-gender groups or if performed in front of mixed audiences. Most primary and secondary schools hold dance in mixed-gender classes and may include popular dance styles, in which movements of the body are seen as sexually expressive and seductive in nature.

At Key Stage 1 and the early phase of Key Stage 2 dance is equated with expressive and creative movements connected with emotions or forces of nature. In this form it would be acceptable to most Muslim pupils and parents.

> However, most Muslim parents will find little or no educational merit or value in dance or dancing after early childhood and may even find it objectionable on moral and religious grounds once children have become sexually mature (puberty). Some parents may consider it to be acceptable within a single-sex context provided the dance movements have no sexual connotations. As dancing is not a normal activity for most Muslim families, Muslim pupils are likely to exhibit reluctance to taking part in it, particularly in mixed-gender sessions. By the same token, dance performances before a mixed gender audience may also be objectionable. (*Towards Greater Understanding: meeting the needs of Muslim pupils in state schools*, Muslim Council of Britain, 2007)

Such positions as these are often supported by scholarly debate centred on the *ahadith* – sayings attributed with greater or lesser certainty to the Prophet or his immediate followers.

To avoid over-burdening the text I will not discuss the relevant *ahadith* here. But to speak with confidence one must have some grasp of these sources of doctrine, so I have included some relevant texts among the books listed in the Resources section.

However, it is fair as a general statement to say that none of the Muslim reservations about the Arts are based on texts from the Qur'an, and that many of the *ahadith* cited are dubious in interpretation or authority.

It is important to bear in mind how marginal these arguments are when we look at the overall picture, and to remember that across the globe most Muslims enjoy a rich artistic experience. Yet as we have seen, in some UK quarters restrictions and even embargoes on the arts are fiercely upheld. Given the lack of real authority for such restrictions, why are they currently so widespread?

There may be an element of rejecting Western culture, asserting identity by seeking the most rigorous forms of Islam. But it may also be because, even if artistic activity itself cannot be proved to be harmful, the arts seem to threaten more general Islamic values:

– Islam emphasises restraint and modesty: the arts are seen as dangerous because they may lead to vainglory, and thence to self-indulgence, sensuality and depravity

– Muslims are enjoined to do nothing in excess, and nothing that distracts from one's religious and social responsibilities: and the arts can too easily become an all-consuming passion, a distraction from the problems of the world

– there is a strong streak of rule-breaking in Western arts traditions: artists are licensed to transgress because this is seen as an integral part of creativity. Yet the essence of Islam is obedience, submission

A precautionary principle is at work – since danger lurks somewhere down the road, it would be safer not even to start the journey. In the article already quoted, Ibrahim Hewitt puts it like this: 'In Islam the time to stop is before you have begun'.

How should arts teachers respond?

It could be argued that there is some validity in these attitudes, that our society is prone to a romanticisation of rule-breaking, transgressive be-haviour, and that this can lead to an indulgence of sexuality, scurrility and obscenity in the arts – sometimes with serious intent, but often shallow and exploitative.

It is perfectly possible to mount a strong defence of artistic transgression: the arts are not a vehicle for morality, but a form of play, and play has powerful psychological benefits not just for children but for people of all ages.

This is fine as long as we know we are just playing, and know when to stop. The problem is that in the present day media-driven and consumerist world, the transgression is often not considered and justified, but merely a knee-jerk conditioned response. We do perhaps need to re-open this debate, because Muslims are not the only group that simply doesn't recognise the notion of the arts as play but insists on a moral agenda.

But let us also recognise that many Muslims, especially the younger genera-tion, have positive attitudes to the arts, value them highly and enjoy them with few qualms. Distinguished scholar Tariq Ramadan argues that to thrive as Europeans, Muslims must make room for the arts in their lives: 'it is not possible to think of a Muslim presence without nourishing and encouraging an artistic and cultural expression which is an alternative to a popular culture that does not often care about ethics or dignity' (Ramadan, 1999).

Thus Ramadan is advocating that Muslims engage with the arts precisely in order to protect themselves from the corrupting effects of the mass media.

There is in fact a struggle going on within the Muslim community. In some areas of the UK, parental and even pupil opposition to certain aspects of the arts curriculum is vocal, even vehement – if often short-lived, as others re-dress the balance and insist on a more tolerant approach.

Yet outside such areas it would be possible for many schools to continue teaching the arts while almost unaware of these struggles. Most Muslim pupils and parents lack the training and experience to make a sustained doc-trinal argument, so they keep their reservations and doubts to themselves, and accept the curriculum they are offered in a compliant spirit. They are naturally reluctant to cause difficulties. They trust the school not to cause their children actual harm. They accept the over-riding value of knowledge even in controversial areas: if their children are to live in the UK, perhaps they do need to know something about its artistic life, even if they themselves are not to get involved. Only occasionally, for instance during the month of Ramadan, when faith issues are at the forefront of every Muslim's mind, do tensions arise in the classroom.

Yet young Muslims often say that they feel uneasy studying music, drama or dance and that they participate only half-heartedly, vaguely aware that what they are doing is wrong. Can we as arts teachers live with this uneasily con-cealed compliance? I suggest not. Surely we want our Muslim pupils to come to value the arts and develop their creativity as fully as any others. So surely we need to engage with Muslim pupils and their parents, to help them think through the issues and move beyond compliance towards endorsement.

As non-Muslim arts teachers we may feel unable to engage in the debate directly, but we must be seen to be listening sympathetically. And we have to project the most positive possible images of the arts to our pupils and parents as they wrestle with these issues. We must not allow the Western arts to be caricatured. After all, most arts practitioners and their followers are models of probity, and most artistic production focuses on worthy, even lofty themes.

We need to stand our ground – UK education for good reason sees the arts as providing important educational benefits, and no-one should be excluded from those. The National Curriculum gives eloquent reasons for making music and art compulsory subjects in the education of all children:

Music is a unique form of communication that can change the way pupils feel, think and act. Music forms part of an individual's identity and positive interaction with music develops pupils' competence as learners and increases their self-esteem. It brings together intellect and feeling and enables personal expression, reflection and emotional development. As an integral part of culture, past and present, music helps pupils understand themselves, relate to others, and develop their cultural understanding, forging important links between the home, school and the wider world.

Music education encourages active involvement in different forms of music making, both individual and communal, helping to develop a sense of group identity and togetherness. Music can influence pupils' development in and out of school; it can help foster personal development and maturity, a sense of achievement and self-worth, and the ability to work with others in a group context.

(QCA – The Secondary Curriculum Review, Programme of Study, Music KS3)

Art and design is a unique way of understanding and responding to the world. It offers opportunities to:

- stimulate children's creativity and imagination by providing visual, tactile and sensory experiences
- develop children's understanding of colour, form, texture, pattern and their ability to use materials and processes to communicate ideas, feelings and meanings
- explore with children ideas and meanings in the work of artists, craftspeople and designers, and help them learn about their different roles and about the functions of art, craft and design in their own lives and in different times and cultures
- help children to learn how to make thoughtful judgements and aesthetic and practical decisions and become actively involved in shaping environments

(DfES – Scheme of Work, Art and Design Key Stages 1 and 2)

Such principles apply equally to the other art forms we teach; indeed many arts teachers take them so for granted that they hardly feel it necessary to mention them. But in a context where the value of the arts is being questioned, we may need to spell out why we see the Arts as essential:

- they are the basis of cultural understanding
- they enable young people to develop their individual identities and personalities
- they are often collaborative, promoting teamwork

- they encourage thinking skills, independent learning and problem solving

- they promote creativity – the ability to discover new ideas

- they are a means of celebrating the beauty and order of the world

- they promote emotional intelligence, helping us understand our feelings and those of others

- they are a gateway to spiritual experience

Most Muslims would place a high value on all these attributes of the arts. And they are particularly important for young people. One reason why the Arts are important is because they go beyond the academic haven into young people's daily lives. They are inextricably part of the social dynamics of the media market-place. That's an exciting place but a dangerous one; yet we do our children no favours by shielding them from it. Rather we need to help them steer their way through the bewildering barrage of the good, the bad and the downright ugly.

What we teach must be more than simply a canon of artistic excellence, a museum culture. Critical appreciation of the work of established artists is important, but it is not enough on its own. Young people need to explore the place of the arts in their own daily lives. And they can only understand the value of the arts through practical engagement, creating their own work and studying the work of others.

The arts can't avoid being contemporary and creative, finding modern meanings in the traditional. They are unthinkable without personal engagement, self-expression.

Anyone who has listened to young Muslims will know how seriously many of them work to define their identity, their place in the world; and how many perplexities they encounter in reconciling the tenets of Islam with their parents' traditional values on the one hand, and the fast-moving, complex secular world of the West on the other. The arts provide a powerful identity-building tool for these young people as they strive for a secure and respected place in the UK.

Because they offer all pupils a chance to express their ideas and to succeed on their own terms, the *Every Child Matters* themes are strongly represented in the arts. Being included and making a contribution enhance self-esteem and are good for emotional wellbeing. So the arts are likely to promote academic motivation and success.

Over two days a group of disaffected Year 9 Muslim boys work with Muslim artist Mohsen Keiany. He shows them how Islamic calligraphy is used to make designs, and how mosques in the Middle East have traditionally been richly decorated with patterns and designs, including the use of stained glass. The boys, used to the more austere atmosphere of UK mosques, are surprised and delighted. They make designs of their own using images suggested by the Middle East – sun, sand, trees and so on; these are treated to create a stained-glass effect. Each pupil copies his design onto a large board, the centre-piece of which is the name of Allah in calligraphy. The end result is a magnificent large-scale piece for display in the school entrance hall. Throughout the two days the boys' behaviour and work-rate have been exemplary.

What I am suggesting here is that every school serving a Muslim community needs to institute a dialogue between teachers on the one hand, and parents, pupils and community leaders on the other. In such a dialogue, the school will show that it is listening, and understands the reservations Muslims have about the arts, but it will seek also to justify and reassure, to assert the value of the arts in all cultures, and to demonstrate familiarity with the rich heritage of Islamic arts.

The majority of parents in a Muslim faith primary school are opposed to the arts aspects of the National Curriculum. Over a period of four years the Head teacher negotiates every aspect of the school curriculum with parents, gradually introducing arts activities, seeking at every stage to explain, per-suade and reassure. These negotiations even embrace the texts of all songs to be learned during the year. The school has recently won an Arts Mark award for the quality and breadth of its provision.

This chapter aims to provide guidance and materials for such a dialogue. I hope the points made here provide a foundation firm enough for you to build on. Other actions that may help are:

–   to research pupil and parent attitudes

–   to stress that the educational context offers children protection from any potentially adverse effects of the Arts

–   to show parents the curriculum in action through workshops, assemblies, displays and classroom visits

A Christian teacher responsible for music in a largely Muslim primary school carries out an extensive piece of action research on the theme of Islam and Music. She studies the literature; explores attitudes among children, parents and fellow teachers through interviews and questionnaires; trials and evaluates some curriculum interventions; and gives Islamic music a high profile through assemblies and a display in the entrance hall. The outcomes are greater trust and understanding between parents and teachers, more confidence among teachers, and a set of policy recommendations for governors.

Strategies for schools and teachers
Ethos

Before considering curriculum or other activities, it is vital to get the ethos right – to create an environment in which young Muslims feel valued and are given space to express themselves and discuss their own issues.

Some key factors in creating this positive ethos include:

- dialogue with young people about Islamic arts issues, listening above all but also demonstrating knowledge and sympathy

- official recognition e.g. playing Islamic music in Assembly

- working with visiting Muslim artists

- providing protected space and time, eg for extra-curricular clubs

- consulting Muslim parents and community leaders, carrying out research into their attitudes and anxieties

- fostering good relationships with Muslim complementary schools (madrasahs)

- recognising and building on the particular arts skills and knowledge the Muslim children bring from beyond the school

In attending classes after school to study Islamic subjects, children acquire a range of experiences and skills which relate to the arts. For instance they learn Arabic letters and words, on which many Muslim visual artists base their work. They learn the stories of the Qur'an; and some of them learn the highly-developed art of reciting or chanting the Qur'an (*tajwid*), which calls for the most delicate control of pitch, rhythm and vocal timbre. We as teachers clearly need to be aware of this learning and show that we value it.

In a girls-only secondary school with Performing Arts College status, teachers are concerned at the lack of involvement of Muslim pupils in the performing arts. For example, dance groups rehearse every lunch time; but the Muslim girls stand around the walls, feeling embarrassed and excluded.

Following a presentation to the whole school, and a meeting with Muslim parents, a group of girls is offered the opportunity to work with Muslim women's arts group Ulfah Arts. About 20 volunteer, drawn from Years 8 to 12.

The project is based on *Quasida Burdah*, the Song of the Cloak, a 13th century devotional poem known throughout the Islamic world. The girls study the text in both Arabic and English translation, and sing passages to the traditional melodies. They talk about the images and meanings of selected passages, and work as a group to write poems expressing these ideas in the language and imagery of their own lives.

They then form small groups to create musical settings of their own poems. One group uses a *nasheed* style, the other blends singing with rap. During the project they have the dance studio to themselves, and start to bring in recordings of *nasheeds* to share.

This is the first time many of these girls have performed for an audience. They are highly motivated by the project, and some are continuing to work with Ulfah Arts outside school.

Having attended an LEA training session, the music specialist in a primary school with a largely Muslim intake has taught children to sing 'Mercy Like the Rain', a setting of a Qur'anic text by Islamic nasheed group Shaam. Children and their parents are surprised and delighted to have this song from their own culture in-cluded; one mother brings into school a recording of the same song as performed in her mosque.

There is a similar delighted response to the use of Islamic music as an introduction to assembly and in music lessons. Children enjoy hearing Gregorian plainchant, in which they recognise many similarities to Islamic music. They also use Islamic calligraphy as a stimulus for abstract musical compositions.

Professional development

In fostering mutual understanding and respect with Muslims, the first and crucial step is to show an interest! But in the longer run a sketchy and super-ficial acquaintance with the field is never going to be enough. Once started on the path, teachers' subject knowledge will become increasingly extensive and deep; but this does not come without effort or happen overnight. We will find ourselves involved in some detailed research, and will want to absorb some of the key techniques through practical experience over a period of time. It is not merely a question of knowing about Islamic methods and achievements in our discipline. We will find ourselves going through a major re-orientation, a change in how we understand and teach our subject. The Islamic approach is less about skills and techniques, more about artistic purposes and values; less about cultures, more about faith and spirituality. Once we start to generate that sort of dialogue in our classrooms, it will lead us to open the doors to Christian, Sikh, Hindu, Buddhist, Jewish artistic values as well – ultimately the implications are vast, and deeply rewarding.

Schemes of work

The next step clearly is to weave Islamic materials and themes into the Arts curriculum – to write appropriate activities into our planning. These will not always take the form of stand-alone units; it is just as important to let Islamic material take a natural place as one example among many of the points we make. In an art lesson we may link work on patterning to the tile patterns in a mosque. A music lesson may include comparisons between the acapella singing of a gospel quartet, an Anglican cathedral choir, and a *nasheed* group. After studying sonnets, young people may experiment with the poetic form of the *ghazal*.

As we have seen, this is not just a matter of introducing new material. It is vital to recognise and discuss the artistic values of Islam and of other faiths, and this will lead us away from How artistic work is created, to asking *Why*. What is the point and purpose of the Arts? Are they just about aesthetics, or do they have social and moral effects as well? This will draw us into talk, writing and reading alongside our practical work. A scheme of work that nourishes Islamic values will have Literacy, Thinking Skills, and Citizenship issues at its core.

> In a Roman Catholic secondary school which includes pupils from other faith backgrounds, the music department has developed a unit of work for Year 9 classes on devotional music of many faiths. Pupils listen to plainsong, Gospel music, and Islamic *qawwali* music, talking about the similarities and differences. They create an abstract instrumental piece based on designs from the Alhambra, aiming for an effect of meditation.

Conclusion

This chapter is advocating that schools engage with the Islamic arts and the views of the Muslim community, and that they adjust their teaching and ethos to include Islamic materials and issues. It would be wrong to see this merely as an obligation imposed on us from above, to alleviate the social and political tensions of the moment. The arts of Islam and the other faiths are powerful and beautiful. They offer rich rewards to pupils and teachers, and arguably we have neglected them for too long.

We have learned over the years to build ethnic cultural elements into our programmes; do we now have to rethink our approach yet again, so that faith becomes more central? The difficulty for UK teachers is that we have largely been brought up in a secular culture, in which religion is marginalised, individuals are free to make their own judgements, and the arts are seen as a form of play. As a result we have tended to avoid discussion of moral and spiritual purposes in the arts, preferring to focus on technical skills: in a phrase, on *doing* rather than *understanding*. Yet we need to recognise that for many people the ethical values of the arts are the prime concern.

For the world is changing. For good and for ill, this new emphasis on faith and spiritual values is here to stay. Artists and Arts teachers have always kept in tune with the way society develops. We are now at the beginning of a major shift in UK culture, a move towards more explicit recognition of spiritual, moral and faith values in society, and therefore in the arts.

This shift may have been hastened by the concerns of Muslims and by the issues surrounding their integration into UK society. But it was coming anyway, and it extends far beyond them. There may be dangers in this new paradigm, but it has also much of value to offer us.

Resources

An extensive reference section can never be complete, and will soon go out of date. Moreover no individual website or book would be accepted by all Muslims as authoritative.

Almost all the artists and thinkers mentioned in this chapter have their own websites; any good search engine will lead you quickly to further information about them, and will show you where to find their work. Similarly, the Internet abounds in information sites and discussion forums, offering the full range of viewpoints. So the Resources section lists only a small selection of texts and websites that are key in helping UK readers to understand the underlying issues.

Books

Association of Muslim Researchers (AMR) (1996) *Much Ado About Music*. London: Education Society of the Association of Muslim Researchers

Behrens-Abousseif D (1990) *Beauty in Arabic Culture*. Princeton: Markus Wiener
A useful guide to scholarly teaching on the role of the arts in Islam set alongside the achievements of the artists themselves

Bunting R (2006) *Muslim Music and Culture in the Curriculum*. Birmingham: Birmingham City Council
Explains the main musical traditions and schools of thought in Islam, with suggestions for curriculum development

Chittick W (2000) *Sufism, A Short Introduction*. Oxford: Oneworld
An understanding of Sufism is central to knowledge of the Islamic arts

Harris, D (2005) *Music and Muslims*. Stoke on Trent: Trentham Books
A fascinating study of the tensions around music among Muslims in the UK and across the world

Muslim Council of Britain (2007) *Towards Greater Understanding: meeting the needs of Muslim pupils in state schools*. London: Muslim Council of Britain

A conservative but moderate Muslim view on ways in which UK schools' ethos and curriculum need to adapt to the needs of children from Muslim families

Ramadan T (1999) *To be a European Muslim.* Leicestershire: The Islamic Foundation

Ramadan T (2004) *Western Muslims and the Future of Islam.* Berkshire: Open University Press
Ramadan is a scholar of great authority, and a powerful voice for rapprochement between Islam and the West

Websites

www.faithandthearts.com (August 2007)
Faith and the Arts
This website set up by Arts Council England is essential reading. The Research Papers and Case Studies are particularly useful in explaining current positions within Islam and other faiths.

www.mcb.org.uk/download/schoolinfoguides.pdf
This section of the website of the Muslim Council of Britain offers a moderate conservative Muslim viewpoint on how state schools might adapt their ethos and curriculum to meet the needs of Muslim pupils, with important discussion of Music, Dance and Performing Arts.

www.sfusd.k12ca.us/schwww/sch618/Islam_New_Main
An outstandingly useful Californian high school site, giving a wealth of information about the historical development of Islamic arts, crafts, recreations, technology and society

4

Every Muslim Child Matters:
Change for children
The five outcomes explained

W e have considered the rationale and processes that underpin a
strategy devoted to meeting the needs of Muslim pupils, emphasis-
ing that the key driver for all services is now *Every Child Matters*
(ECM). Central government departments and centrally funded bodies like the
Department for Children, Schools and Families (DCSF), the Department of
Health, Ofsted and the QCA; local government services like Children and
Young People's Services, Learning and Skills Councils, Connexions, Social
Care and Health, Housing and the schools themselves – everybody working
with young people has to address the five key outcomes and everybody is inspected against them. The framing of this agenda has changed utterly, and
now completely dominates the landscape for children. All children should be
healthy, should stay safe, should enjoy and achieve, should make a positive
contribution and should achieve economic wellbeing.

Within each of the five outcomes, there are particular issues that are relevant
to Muslim pupils. For the outcomes to be successfully realised everyone involved must take Muslim perspectives into account. This chapter examines
each outcome and provides questions to guide schools and services to meet
Muslim needs more effectively. The questions themselves form a useful tem-
plate for service self evaluation.

Every Muslim Child Matters – Change for Children
Outcome 1 – Being healthy

Being healthy: commentary from Muslim perspectives

Being Healthy underpins all the other ECM outcomes, for without good physical and emotional health young people are unlikely to enjoy school, achieve highly and, ultimately, do well in the world of work. 'Being healthy' involves five major themes:

- children and young people are physically healthy
- children and young people are mentally and emotionally healthy
- children and young people are sexually healthy
- children and young people live healthy lifestyles
- children and young people choose not to take illegal drugs

As good Muslims, parents, carers and young people can identify with these overarching aims. But they will expect schools to exhibit a great deal of sensitivity, as issues of sex and sexuality go to the very heart of some Muslims' negative perceptions of non-Islamic western society. One problem is that while the Islamic perspectives in some areas of health are very clear, they are ambiguous in others.

Perhaps because of their generally low socio-economic status, Muslims have the highest rates of ill-health, after allowances are made for the distinction of different age groups in the community. Dr Shahid, writing in MCB Direct (2004) reports the *Sickening State of Muslim Health in Britain*. As well as physical health, he is concerned about what he calls 'the appalling rate of disability among Muslims'. Roughly a quarter of Muslim women and a fifth of Muslim men indicated that they had a limiting long-term illness or disability which restricted their daily activities; the highest for any religious group in Britain. Similarly, the DfES (2006) reported that pupils of Pakistani and Bangladeshi origin are two to two and a half times as likely as white British pupils to be identified as having profound and multiple learning difficulties, a visual impairment, hearing impairment or multi-sensory impairment.

Speculation as to the causes of such comparatively high incidence of profound and multiple learning difficulties leads to the hugely sensitive issue of consanguinity (where parents are blood relations, often first cousins). The literature suggests genetic factors, but great care has to be taken not to over-attribute developmental difficulties to this factor. Consanguinity is not common to all Muslim societies and may be more cultural than religious. Cousin marriage, however, is not prohibited in Islam. Indeed Muhammad (PBUH) married his daughter Fatima to his own cousin, Ali and this has been taken as approval of the practice. However, the context of the time (Islam was in its infancy and there were few adherents) is not always taken into account. Other Muslims cite sources which encourage marriage outside the family circle. Regardless of the religious position taken it is clear that this has the potential to be a very worrying issue for young Muslim men and women.

There is, however, no issue about the place of sport in Islam. Muslims are enjoined by the Qur'an to keep fit and encouraged to take part in physical activities such as swimming, archery and horse riding. Keeping fit is part of the Islamic way of life. What concerns many parents, however, are where the activities take place, with whom and who might be watching. A key Islamic principle for both boys and girls is the principle of modesty, *haya*, which is defined as 'to encompass notions of modesty, humility, decency and dignity' (MCB 2007). It applies to all aspects of life but is particularly relevant in terms of changing facilities – which ought to be separate in primary as well as secondary schools – in girls having their arms and legs covered and, as girls enter puberty, separate swimming arrangements.

Swimming and PE may not be problematic. Dance, however, can be. Some Muslims see popular dance as 'sexually expressive and seductive in nature' (MCB 2007) and obviously inconsistent with Islamic notions of *haya*, especially when it involves physical contact in mixed gender groups, and in front of mixed audiences. The health and educational benefits of dance are not always clearly explained to parents and although there is no right to opt out of these lessons, schools are encouraged to be sensitive and respect the religious convictions of parents and carers.

The greatest potential minefield, however, comes in the teaching about Sex and Relationships Education (SRE). Marital sex is seen as healthy, for both procreation and pleasure. Any sex outside marriage is *haram* (forbidden) and is seen as destructive to the essential Islamic position of the sanctity of marriage as the bedrock of the family and society. The Islamic position concerning homosexuality is similarly explicit – that too is *haram*. That said, Muslims are encouraged to be caring to those with homosexual tendencies in the hope that they might overcome such desires, not drive them out or persecute them.

There is no prohibition of sex education for Muslims providing it is age appropriate, and is about teaching young people to relate to others in ways which are consistent with Islamic moral values and principles. As the MCB puts it, 'sex education should provide factual information objectively and educate young people to look forward to adult life with a sense of responsibility, accountability and happiness and be ready to build a strong, stable family life'. For them, like most Muslims, SRE is about helping young people 'to understand the different sexual values and behaviours they will observe within a pluralist society'. For Muslim parents the key word is 'observe', not take part in. Helping young people control their 'illicit' sexual urges is part of the struggle, the *jihad*, against their baser selves, as it distracts them from the proper remembrance of God.

In the perception of some Muslim parents it is not the principle but the content of the SRE syllabus and the methods and teaching aids used that can cause deep offence, as they feel the subject can encourage lascivious thought. Explicit videos and diagrams, discussions in mixed gender groups, the open and free discussion around these issues, can be seen as inappropriate and harmful. The very wording of the ECM outcome about being sexually healthy can also be a cause for concern because it appears to be predicated on an acceptance that young people will be sexually active regardless of their marital status, an acceptance that is anathema to practising Muslims. It is difficult growing up in such an overtly sexual environment, and sometimes requires a saintly temperament to avoid temptation. Few are blessed with such a temperament, and as growing Muslim teenage pregnancy rates reveals, Muslims are as likely as any other group to succumb to worldly vices. All the more reason to actively avoid temptation in SRE wherever possible.

Intoxicants, including illicit drugs, and gambling must also be avoided. The position concerning cigarette smoking is less clear. Some scholars argue that it is permissible, and others claim that it is not. There is no such confusion about other drugs and alcohol. The Qur'anic injunction is clear: '*Satan's plan is to excite enmity and hatred between you with intoxicants and gambling and hinder you from the remembrance of Allah and from prayer, will you not then abstain?*' (5:90). Unfortunately a growing number of young Muslims find it difficult to abstain from drug taking and, in some cases, drug trafficking. As the Muslim Health Network (www.muslimhealthnetwork.org) puts it:

> Over the last decade drug use has been gradually increasing within the Muslim community. In some areas it has reached crisis point and some are still under the impression that it is not an issue within the community. In the long term a single drug user has an impact upon the whole community. Yet, with virtually no Islamically oriented treatment options available and with very few Muslims skilled in drug related work, Muslim parents are often left in a state of confusion. Nevertheless, they are often the first ones who seek help for their son's or daughter's drug use!

The issue for many Muslim parents is that, whereas alcohol abuse has always been a feature of human life, they can be ignorant about the different types of drugs available to young people and are often unaware of the physical signs of drug use. Similarly, they are often unaware of the emotional traumas that can lead young people to substance abuse.

They, like most of their non-Muslim counterparts, are unlikely to be aware of the language and concepts that surround the issues related to emotional and spiritual health and their crucial importance in identity formation. Identity, however, is a complex and complicated concept in the age in which we live. Young British Muslims will be influenced by western culture, by peer culture, by the cultural backgrounds of their parents, and of course by their faith. These influences can be contradictory and confusing, especially perhaps for Muslims children. It can be extremely hard to unpick aspects that are driven by culture, as opposed to those which are faith driven. This becomes particularly relevant for those who might be attracted to radical Islam. Even for those who are not, it is difficult for young Muslims growing up in Britain because the values of their parents, especially in relation to mixing with members of the opposite sex may conflict with the general freedoms enjoyed by young people.

These conflicts can take extreme forms when issues of family honour (known as *izzat*) is seen to be at stake. At its most extreme *izzat* has led to high profile 'family honour' killings. It is highly likely that this is one of the underlying causes of the rise in the suicide rate amongst 16-24 year old Asian women, reportedly three times that of white British women in the same age group. Shaista Gohir, writing in the *Islamic Times* in July 2007 (www.islamictimes.co.uk/content/view/662/50/) added the hugely contentious issue of patient confidentiality as another possible cause. Many Asian and Muslim women, he argued, are reluctant to talk to health professionals about problems facing them because they fear the information would be relayed back to their families. This has repercussions for young people as they too must believe that any sensitive matters discussed with professionals will remain strictly confidential and not be communicated to their parents.

For young people growing up in the 21st century, especially for those whose parents were born elsewhere, the world can appear a very confused and confusing place. Our early multicultural identity paradigms tended to be binary. We spoke of 'between two' cultures, or a clash of cultures, especially where there appeared to be major differences between the culture of the new arrival and the 'host'. The present paradigm is much more complicated.

Young people now have plural or multiple identities and these identities shift according to the context. Thus, young British born Muslims might emphasise their religious background in one setting, their cultural background in another, their 'racial' identity in a third. Each of these has its own narrative and its own stories that provide meaning. Unlike many other groups however, the key determinant in the formation of these multiple identities is the Islamic faith.

The implications of pupils' multiple identities for teaching and learning and for Children's Services are profound. If we want to secure services that allow young Muslims to be healthy they must feel valued and be encouraged to develop positive relationships across all backgrounds. So it is essential that young people be given the space to express their values openly without fear of recrimination, even when these values differ or even conflict with those of the mainstream. It is equally essential that, within this supportive framework, young people are taught to be reflectively self-critical. Such approaches will help build what Ostberg has called 'an integrated plural identity,' an identity which allows a young person to feel safe and secure in a variety of different settings.

For Muslim pupils to become emotionally and spiritually healthy, they must feel that their faith background is acknowledged in all educational settings. They must be supported to become 'skilled cultural and faith navigators' (Coles *et al*, 2006), aware of their own identities and willing and able to engage empathetically with others. The considerable work in what is now called *emotional literacy* should help all pupils. But the area of spiritual literacy is much less developed. This is especially true of the vibrant Islamic spiritual tradition where links have yet to be made between mainstream schooling and the rich literature of the Sufi tradition (Coles *et al*, 2006).

The influence of parents is as crucial if not more crucial than that of the school, especially when it comes to the transmission of faith. The Joseph Rowntree report, (Cassen and Kingdom, 2007) argues that although schools do make a difference to outcomes, about 14 per cent of the incidence of low attainment is attributable to school quality. The inference is clear: 86 per cent of low attainment is attributable to wider socio-economic factors related to the pupils' home and communities. An interesting finding when you consider that pupils are estimated to spend only 15 per cent of their time in school and 85 per cent outside. The implications for parent education are profound. The DfES in their *Every Parent Matters* (2007) acknowledges this in no uncertain terms: 'The evidence that good parenting plays a huge role in educational attainment is too compelling to ignore. It outstrips every other single factor including social class, ethnicity or disability – in its impact on attainment'.

Heralding a major change of policy, the document outlines a range of measures the government intends to implement support for parents in various settings. The Islamic perspectives on parenting are unequivocal. The salaam-Muslim information resource site (www.salaam.co.uk) encapsulates this perspective:

> Islam wants all human beings to grow up as emissaries of Allah on earth. In that respect, parenting in Islam is a divine responsibility. Parental duty is at the heart of Muslim life. For a sound and healthy continuity of Islamic civilisation every parent has to transfer the spirit and message of Islam to their offspring. If an individual parent cannot cope with this great and demanding task for some reason, the community has to create such network that nobody in the *ummah* falls through the net.

This divine responsibility applies to fathers as much as mothers. The debate the Muslim community has been having about the place of fathers in bringing up their children mirrors much of *Every Parent Matters*. Amongst others, the An-Nisa society in conjunction with Fathers Direct and *Q news* has campaigned to raise the profile of this issue. The research indicates that some fathers experience communication difficulties with their children, especially adolescents, who may have been brought up in a society with very different social norms to their own. Fathers can react negatively and sometimes violently to their perceived loss of respect and authority. Narrow, circumscribed traditional roles are not suited to the lifestyles of Muslims in the UK. The work of organisations like An-Nisa and Fathers Direct is vital in supporting fathers in coming to terms with the changing nature of their role.

Being healthy: questions from Muslim perspectives

Have Muslim pupils the opportunity to

- pray if they wish?

- pray in a clean and dedicated place?

- pray after their ritual ablution (*wudu*)?

- explore their spirituality from a Muslim perspective?

- engage in faith based dialogue with people of other faiths and those of no faith?

- undertake PE, sports, movement and dance in a manner which is generally Islamically acceptable?

- undertake school performance in a manner which is Islamically acceptable?

- undertake collective worship in a way that will not offend?

- undertake Sex and Relationships Education without offence, and not during Ramadan?

- eat healthy *halal* or vegetarian meals that have been prepared and cooked in a prescribed manner?

- fast during Ramadan, and enjoy warmth and security during lunch breaks?

- wear Islamically acceptable clothing, whilst adhering to Health and Safety directives?

- relate to people with whom they can confide freely and in strict confidence about sensitive issues related to, for example their identity, sexuality, potential marriage partner, and consanguinity?

- be sure that whatever they say in private will be treated with total confidentiality?

- know where to go and what to do if they suffer bullying?

- behave in a way which supports their identity as people of faith?

- behave in such away that will discourage criminal behaviours?

- speak openly and freely about all the 'being healthy' issues?

- be consulted formally and informally about how the schools should respond to these issues?

Are Muslim parents:

- clearly informed about their child's progress and future prospects?

- encouraged to take an active part in school life?

- encouraged to learn about healthy eating?

- encouraged to learn about illicit drugs?

- encouraged – especially fathers – to learn about parenting skills?

Every Muslim Child Matters – Change for Children
Outcome 2 – Staying Safe

Staying safe: commentary from Muslim perspectives

Much of the original impetus for *Every Child Matters* came from some high profile cases involving system failures in dealing with seriously abused children. In 2003 the government published a green paper, *Every Child Matters*, a alongside the formal response to the report into the death of Victoria Climbié; the young girl who was horrifically abused, tortured and killed by her great aunt and the man with whom they lived. The focus of the green paper was very much on supporting families and carers, ensuring early intervention and improving service integration with the core objective of safeguarding young people in all settings. Serious debate amongst service providers, schools and young people themselves has, as expected, significantly widened the Staying Safe agenda. It urges that

- children and young people be safe from maltreatment, neglect, violence and sexual exploitation

- children and young people be safe from accidental injury and death

- children and young people be safe from bullying and discrimination

- children and young people be safe from crime and anti-social behaviour in and out of school

- children and young people have security, stability and be cared for

There are two major developing areas that require discussion: being safe from types of harm and being safe to undertake a range of activities without fear of negative consequences. Muslim perspectives on most of the staying safe issues will be the same as those of any other group as Islam places great store on the sanctity of the family and expressly condemns crime, anti-social behaviour and any form of discrimination and exploitation.

There are several areas, however, where Muslims are more vulnerable than others. Racial bullying is common to many, Islamophobia is not. All the evidence indicates that after any major terrorist incident, there is a dramatic increase in Islamophobia. The language of some newspapers and other media becomes inflammatory and can raise tensions and ill feeling. The war and continued occupation in Iraq and other aspects of British foreign policy can be a cause for concern and friction; schools and local authorities need to be sensitive to possible tensions. Some have adopted policies on dealing with sensitive and contentious issues which provide guidelines to help institutions in difficult times.

Work remains to be done, however, about the nature of guidance and support to schools in tackling Islamic extremism. The major problem is that discussion about this issue tends to be discouraged, goes underground and schools are understandably reluctant to involve themselves in any debate. The atmosphere is, however, changing and the position of openness and of condemning terror taken originally by the MCB is now becoming the norm. Young Muslims need to feel secure enough to be able to raise these issues in school, either in appropriate lessons or with a trusted adult. Each outrage raises tensions within the community and Muslim pupils must feel able to talk openly in school without fear of being labelled a 'terrorist.' The Muslim community generally is becoming increasingly aware that one key way of addressing extremism is to become actively involved in the debate, to use their own Muslim frame of reference to demonstrate the essential balance of Islam.

The Radical Middle Way Project, for example, 'is a Muslim grassroots initiative aimed at articulating a mainstream understanding of Islam that is dynamic, pro-active and relevant, particularly to young British Muslims. It is managed by young British Muslims themselves, in a partnership between FOSIS, Mahabba Unlimited, *Q News* and YMOUK. The project has its roots in Islamic history, being an organic response by traditional Islam to challenges posed by extremist ideas. The project seeks to combat ignorance by spreading and empowering arguments for a 'middle way'.

Their website (www.radicalmiddleway.co.uk) opens with a quote explicitly declaring their position from the outset. Reporting a speech by Shaykh Ali al-Jifri on principled behaviour and the essential nature of balance in Islam they state:

> Do not be afraid in this country. You are a part of it. Feel that you have a responsibility towards improving it and remedying its ailments. If you see good, follow it through, and if you see wrong, be the first to reject it. If someone wants to do harm to the country in the name of Islam, we are the first to reject him

The Nasiha Bradford Citizenship Project in mosques and madrasahs, which aims to introduce the teaching of citizenship in madrasahs, is a brave step in a similar direction but has not been universally welcomed by all Muslim groups, who can see it as the heavy hand of the state interfering in their religious affairs. Many local authorities and individual schools do, however, enjoy a good working relationship with the madrasahs and are increasingly concerned to ensure that pupils attending are safe, and that they enjoy a good learning experience whilst they are on the premises.

The same is true for Muslim pupils who are fostered or looked after in care homes. 'Why do Muslim children in care need Muslim foster homes?' The website www.fostercarelink.com offers a short but clear analysis of the importance of the Islamic frame of reference. This analysis is also relevant to all young Muslims looked after by the local authorities.

The increasing number of young Muslims getting into serious trouble with the police indicates that are not 'staying safe.' Dr Basia Spalek's article 'Muslims in British Prisons' (www.hmprisonservice.gov.uk) paints a grim picture of the increase in Muslim inmates. Muslims make up over 10 per cent of the prison population but only 3 per cent of the overall population. The peak age for committing a detected offence is 18 for males and 15 for females.

Much of the literature concentrates on what happens to Muslims in prisons, the nature of the support and the rehabilitation. Little attention has been given to the causes of this increase and the preventative measures schools and local authorities might adopt. There is a great sense of shame in Muslim families if one of their own is incarcerated and often great reluctance even to talk about what has happened. The www.muslimyouth.net, are, however are addressing the issue head on. Their 'Ramadan Behind Bars Campaign' is now an annual event. Citing the *hadith*, 'Help the wrongdoer and one that is wronged,' they are raising the profile of both the causes and the effects of criminalisation:

> Unfortunately many first generation Muslim parents and elders can simply not relate to, nor understand some of the problems faced by many Muslim youth today, and subsequently choose to ignore or worse cover up this increasingly widespread taboo. (www.myh.org.uk/services.php?id=4).

There are serious implications for schools, local authorities and youth offending teams. The need to address what appears to be a growing problem, in terms of both prevention and rehabilitation.

Staying safe: questions from Muslim perspectives

Are Muslim pupils safe from

- Islamophobia?

- racial and other forms of bullying?

- the effects of crime and anti-social behaviour?

- the effects of the lure of criminal sub culture?

- the effects of negative stereotyping by individuals, the media and other institutions?

- the effects of extremist Islamic ideologies?

- the effects of a secular and liberal society which is perceived to be at odds with Islamic values?

Are Muslim pupils safe to

- learn freely in an encouraging atmosphere?

- speak openly about their faith?

- speak openly about their cultural backgrounds and personal family histories?

- speak openly about issues of terror?

- speak openly about Islamophobia?

- speak openly about issues of gender and sexuality?

- speak openly about issues of marriage?

- practise their religious observances at school (such as fasting, under-taking *wudu* and praying)

- observe and celebrate their major religious festivals, like Eid?

- wear the headscarf?

- effectively observe the principles of modesty like covering the legs, showering separately and not undertaking mixed PE or swimming?

- bring their learning from the madrasahs back into mainstream?

- undertake residential trips?

Are Muslim pupils safe

- at school and en-route to and from school?

- at madrasahs and en-route to and from madrasahs?

- at home – especially if expressing views or acting in a way which may offend parents or community sensitivity?

- in their foster or care homes?

Every Muslim Child Matters – Change for Children
Outcome 3 – Enjoy and Achieve

Enjoy and achieve: commentary from a Muslim perspective

The a*hadith*, 'seeking knowledge is compulsory for every Muslim, man and woman,' and 'seek knowledge even unto China,' are probably two of the most famous in the Muslim world. There is a wonderful Arabic proverb which states, 'Buy books and write down knowledge, for weather is transitory, but knowledge is lasting' (al-Hassani S T S, 2006). With the many explicit exhortations in praise of education Muslims ought to be among our highest achievers.

For a number of reasons, however, they are not. Many Muslims pupils whose parents or grandparents emigrated from the Indian sub-continent and who are now second or third generation are still amongst the lowest achievers. Although the statistical situation is difficult to unpack as DCSF figures are based upon ethnicity rather than religion, and attainment varies between and within regions, the DCSF annual publication, *Ethnicity and Education: The evidence on minority ethnic pupils aged 3-16*, concludes that Pakistani and Bangladeshi origin pupils have constantly performed below the average for all pupils on every scale of the Foundation Stage profile; and that Pakistani and Bangladeshi origin pupils consistently have lower levels of attainment than most other ethnic groups across all key stages . They also make less progress at primary school. Similarly, and most worrying of all, 31 per cent of British Muslims leave school with no qualifications compared to 15 per cent of the total population.

At one level it is difficult to reconcile the positive Islamic view of education with the attainment statistics. Why, if Islam rates education for both boys and girls so highly, are levels of attainment below national averages? It is probably true that the Pakistani and Bangladeshi communities generally came from the poorer and least well educated parts of the sub-continent and tended to take the least well paid jobs in British society. Many came from rural parts and their knowledge of Islam was not particularly well developed. Like other rural communities emigrating to a very different land, this experience often entrenched very conservative attitudes, especially when it came to the education and position of girls. Culture rather than faith,or a cultural interpretation of faith, has not helped the Muslim community to attain highly.

The Enjoy and Achieve outcome aims to address the issue of underachievement and is predicated on the premise that if children enjoy school they are more likely to do well, pass exams and go on to achieve in the world of work.

Christine Gilbert, Her Majesty's Chief Inspector of Schools, adds another dimension in her annual report 2005/06

> Pupils enjoy and achieve when they can see the relevance of what they are learning to their own lives, and it is in these circumstances that subjects such as citizenship, geography, religious education, and personal, social and health education are at their most compelling. (Ofsted, 2006)

'Relevance', especially within an Islamic frame of reference, can support attainment. Given also that so many Muslim pupils come from linguistic backgrounds where community languages like Urdu, Bengali and Gujarati, are spoken at home, it is likely to add to pupils' enjoyment if these languages are encouraged at school. The same is true of Arabic for, whilst not normally a heritage language, its centrality to Islam means that every Muslim has some basic understanding of the language. Enjoy and Achieve has five aims:

- children and young people are ready for school

- children and young people attend and enjoy school

- children and young people achieve stretching national educational standards at primary school

- children and young people achieve personal and social development and enjoy recreation

- children and young people achieve stretching national educational standards at secondary school

The thrust is generally on achieving rather than enjoying, and even more specifically on attaining which relates to that which can be measured by examinations like SATs and GCSEs. Achievement is a broad concept and can include effort, progress, attitudes and a whole range of skills that are not normally formally measured. It can be difficult to distinguish between achieve and enjoy as they tend to coalesce.

In their analysis of 75 local authorities' Children and Young People's Plans, The National Foundation for Education Research (www.nfer.ac.uk) found that overall, enjoyment is chiefly aligned with recreation rather than with learning. Enjoyment relates to activities and strategies connected with play and the development of a coordinated play and recreation policy. This in turn can lead to wider development of family strategies and family workshops, based in Children's Centres and a range of extended services. Many authorities and schools do support the Ready for school aim by improving access to, and take up of, family and parent support, including, for instance, advice and guidance, health and counselling, and workshops on parenting skills.

Some authorities place the emphasis on enjoyment with '*learning to learn, loving to learn,*' and the development of creative approaches across the curriculum as key objectives (NFER 2007). Schools and Local Authorities are more secure in their attempts to achieve 'stretching national educational standards at primary and secondary school', especially as we now have a number of more sophisticated tools to support data analysis and intervention strategies, such as Raise on Line and Context Value Added.

As Robert Vincent clearly explains in his article (2007), schools and Local Authorities can now target underachieving groups and individuals with enormous precision, and can devise a range of measures to address provision. In addition, the QCA curriculum changes can be used as an opportunity to be more responsive to personalised learning needs. Personal and social development and recreation can likewise support a broad and balanced curriculum including sport and arts based activities, both within school and in partnership with other agencies. It is now more than possible to construct a curriculum that supports Muslim identity, acknowledges and celebrates faith and encourages pupils to both enjoy and achieve.

Enjoy and achieve: questions from Muslim perspectives

In terms of being ready for school and attending and enjoying it whilst they are there,

- do your Muslim pupils attend and enjoy school? How do you know?

- what support, training and advice do you offer Muslim parents so that their children are ready for school?

- do you offer any particular training to parents that utilise the Muslim frame of reference to support young Muslims in their endeavours throughout compulsory education?

- do you encourage Muslim parents to be open about their perception of the education offered?

- are the parents aware of the importance that Islam places on education, and aware how they might support their children in understanding something of the Muslim heritage and experience?

- do your home-school workers have an understanding of the Muslim frame of reference?

■ are your Muslim pupils aware of their Muslim heritage and do you use it so that pupils might enjoy school more?

■ are your Muslim pupils comfortable in school with their Islamic identity?

■ are Muslim pupils represented on school councils and other participating bodies?

■ do your Muslim pupils see their faith perspective reflected in the general life of the school, its corridors, displays, curriculum and celebrations?

■ do your Muslim pupils talk about what they have learnt in madrasahs, and do they relate it to their mainstream learning?

In terms of achieving stretching national educational standards at primary and secondary school, do you

■ use data effectively so you can chart the progress of your Muslim pupils against national targets?

■ identify with precision their attainment and their progress and implement intervention and support programmes to support them?

■ identify any issues of attendance, and address them?

■ take steps to ensure as much continuity of educational provision, if Muslim pupils take extended holidays in their heritage countries?

■ provide school work and electronic twinning if pupils are abroad for some time?

■ monitor the total curriculum you offer to ensure that the Muslim heritage and experience is adequately covered?

■ ensure that Muslim perspectives permeate the curriculum offer?

■ promote the use and, where appropriate, the formal examination of heritage languages like Urdu, Gujarati and Bengali?

■ teach or support the teaching of Arabic, especially Qur'anic Arabic?

■ attempt to form close links with the mosques and madrasahs so that the learning is mutually re-enforced by school and supplementary education?

■ encourage the teaching and learning of Islamic studies?

■ encourage discussion about some of the more contentious issues related to Islam?

Every Muslim Child Matters – Change for Children
Outcome 4 – Make a Positive Contribution

Make a positive contribution: commentary from Muslim perspectives

There are five key aims in outcome 4, 'make a positive contribution':

■ engage in decision-making and support the community and environment

■ engage in law-abiding and positive behaviour in and out of school

■ develop positive relationships and choose not to bully and discriminate

■ develop self-confidence and successfully deal with significant life changes and challenges

■ develop enterprising behaviour

The Government does not define 'positive contribution' but it is clearly connected with 'active citizenship' and 'civic participation'. One key criticism is that the wording of the objectives can be seen as intrinsically deficient, as a negative construct that is more about social control, about responsibilities more than about rights. But there is much that is positive about the positive contribution and, in many ways, the overarching aims appear almost tailor made for Muslims as both the Qur'an and the *Sunnah* contain numerous exhortations to treat all mankind with active kindness, regardless of their faith or non-faith background.

Indeed one of the five pillars is *zakat*, the giving of alms which requires Muslims to give a portion of their wealth to support the poor. Sharing and caring is a duty for all adherents. The Prophet said that, 'no one amongst you attains true Faith until he likes for his brother what he likes for himself'. Islam is and always has been an active religion. Indeed, worship must be accompanied by service; pious lip-service divorced from action will never make a good Muslim. For Muslims 'faith in action' is the key, and words without practice (*Ihsan*) hollow.

The evidence we have of the views and actions of young British Muslims, though relatively limited, is that most of them are more than keen to actively practice their faith, keen to make a positive contribution within their English context. For example, *Faithful and Proud,* the report of the 120 16-19 year old

British Muslims at the conference held in Leicester in September 2005 demonstrated that young Muslims wanted to integrate into British society whilst retaining their strong Islamic faith and believed that such integration was compatible with their faith. They were proud to be British and Muslim. They were reflective and honest about themselves but critical of political processes, which they did not understand and from which they felt excluded. Crucially, they wanted help and support to become actively involved in these processes as they were very keen to help their own and other communities (*Faithful and Proud* www.sdsa.net 2006).

These findings were consistent with the results of a number of faith based focus groups undertaken on behalf of the Institute of Community Cohesion, for the Department of Communities and Local Government. The report, *Faith, interfaith and cohesion: the education dimension* (SDSA October 2006 www.coventry.ac.uk/icoco/a/264) was based upon an extensive review of materials, products, processes and organisations that have been designed to promote community cohesion and interfaith collaboration. The young people's focus groups followed a pattern of organisation which brought together young people of one faith with others of different or no faith, The Muslims were key to both the Oldham and the Bradford encounters. They, like all faith groups represented, were keen to work together on specific, concrete projects that would benefit all members of the communities they served. They wanted a series of structured interfaith activities that permitted genuine interaction which, they believed, would lead to mutual understanding.

The conclusions of both reports were echoed in a systematic survey undertaken for Gallup and reported by *The Times* under the headline, 'Poll reveals Muslims as model citizens.' (*The Times*, April 2007). The findings are part of a global survey of Muslim attitudes carried out by Gallup, which conducted face to face interviews with individuals aged 15 and over in 40 Muslim countries. Dalia Mogahead, executive director of the Gallup Centre for Muslim Studies was responsible for interviewing 500 Muslims and 1200 members of the UK general public in 2006. She found that 'some of the most striking insights are that religious and national identities are complementary in the UK and high religiosity amongst London Muslims does not translate into sympathy for radicalisation' (www.gallupworld.com). London Muslims generally agreed with the British public that mastering the national language, getting a better education, finding a job, participating in politics, volunteering to serve the public, and celebrating national holidays are necessary for successful integration. Imam Abduljalil Sajid welcomed the results of the poll, highlighting the encouraging extent of Muslim involvement in donating to charities and volunteering and Muslim recognition of democratic institutions. He said that they indicated the extent of Muslim integration and provided an example for other countries (www.christianmuslimforum.org).

That is not to say that the picture is uniformly positive. Far from it. There is serious disaffection amongst many young Muslims, disaffection that could undermine attempts to foster cohesion and could discourage young Muslims from making a positive contribution. Darcus Howe, in a highly contentious Channel 4 programme, '*Who you calling a nigger?*' screened in April 2004, revealed a worrying picture of inter-ethnic tensions in Walsall between youths of Pakistani and African Caribbean origin. The programme provoked outrage from many minority ethnic and Muslim groups (www.blink.org.uk) who felt that it was highly tendentious, overstated the negativity and could cause serious harm to community relations.

These tensions did however come to the fore in Lozells, Birmingham in October 2005, with several days of disturbances that resulted in two deaths. In their comprehensive report of the disturbances commissioned by Birmingham City Council, Black Radley offered a comprehensive yet cautionary analysis of the antecedents and a series of recommendations (www. black radley.com May 2007). The report points out that these disturbances were very different from those that broke out in the northern cities of England in 2001, and totally different from the major rioting that took place in the area in 1986.

As always with such events, a number of factors – social, economic, cultural, drugs, youth – come together to form an explosive cocktail. The distinction between the religious and the cultural factors tends to be blurred but the majority Asian involvement, by virtue of the fact that the population is largely Pakistani or Kashmiri, was Muslim. Amongst its many recommendations the report argues for a greater celebration of the achievements of young people, and an awareness raising programme. As the report put it, 'Racism amongst white people has become socially unacceptable in almost any setting, as a result of awareness raising and a shift in attitudes over the last 30 years. A similar programme should be implemented with Black Minority Ethnic groups as its target market.'

Youth Services could have a crucial role to play in such a programme, especially for those aged 13-19. They also have a vital role in supporting young Muslims to make a positive contribution in areas like citizenship and community participation. Youth Service provision involves galvanising young people to take an active part in youth councils or forums, youth action and other projects designed to identify and respond to local needs, peer education and volunteering. Central government policy documents like *Youth Matters* (DfES 2005), and *Hear by Right* (DfES 2005), especially when augmented with funds drawn from the Youth Opportunity Fund or Youth Capital Fund, provided a structured framework to support participation in many areas including sport and volunteering.

Make a positive contribution: questions from Muslim perspectives

How do you encourage young Muslims to engage in decision making, support the community and environment and live their faith in action? Are they

- involved in School Councils and other forms of policy and democracy?

- participating in School Council and other types of election?

- involved in commenting on the school's SEF?

- involved in inputting into the school's improvement plan?

- involved in fund-raising and other projects that support the local environment?

- involved in inter faith activities?

- involved in the appropriate governing bodies and election to Young People's Parliament?

- involved in workforce appointment panels?

How do you encourage young Muslims to develop positive relationships and choose not to bully and discriminate? For example, do you

- support young Muslims in their interfaith activities?

- encourage them to discuss issues that might cause conflict amongst themselves or between other groups?

- help them become more aware of the underlying issues that relate to radicalisation and terror?

- offer a programme of structured twinning with other groups, both virtual and actual?

- use Islamic perspectives to unpick attitudes towards gender and sexual orientation?

- use Islamic values to stress the Prophet's message of common humanity overlaid with a genuine concern for all God's creatures?

- help young Muslims to unravel some of the complex issues of habits and customs that are culturally driven as opposed to faith driven?

- confront some of the negative stereotypes that exist within Muslim communities?

- offer young Muslims the opportunity to provide mentoring support to others, using their Muslim obligation of tolerance?

How do you develop self-confidence and help them deal with significant life changes and challenges? For example, do you

- ensure that the school curriculum does reflect the experiences and heritage of Muslim pupils in as many curricular areas as possible?

- engage in curriculum development that both involves Muslim pupils, encourages their faith perspectives and fulfils statutory requirements?

- celebrate, the achievements that Muslim pupils have made in madrasahs and in mosques, in the normal course of school life?

- validate and encourage young Muslims to use their faith perspective in discussions and decision making processes?

- celebrate and effectively utilise their linguistic achievements and developments in areas like the Arabic, Urdu, Gujarati, Turkish and other community languages?

- offer confidential counselling to Muslims, who may be undergoing conflict related to expectations about their role as women, their sexual orientation, or 'forced marriages'?

How do you develop enterprising behaviour in young Muslims? For example, do you

- use Muslim role-models to inspire enterprise?

- provide space for young people to discuss and understand ethical banking, Muslim objections to certain types of non-Muslim banking?

- use the new PSHE programme of study – Personal Wellbeing, Economic Wellbeing and Financial Capabilities – to support Muslim pupils to develop enterprising behaviour?

How do you help Muslims engage in law-abiding and positive behaviour in and around school? For example do you

- use the key aspects of Islamic ethics, in particular those related to social responsibilities in stressing good behaviour?

- use the concept of *adab* to reinforce this?

- provide a safe space to discuss issues related to Muslims in prisons?

- offer young offenders adequate support after serving their sentences?

Every Muslim Child Matters – Change for Children
Outcome 5 – Achieve Economic Wellbeing

Achieve economic wellbeing: commentary from Muslim perspectives

The National Youth Agency research programme series provides an excellent analysis of all five themes of Every Child Matters from a Youth Service perspective. Their book *Economic Wellbeing: The Implication for Youth Work for ECM* (2007) offers an astute critique of this theme:

> Economic wellbeing underpins all the other themes in Every Child Matters since its corollary, economic disadvantage (or relative poverty) links life chances, increasing the risk of ill-health, creating a barrier to developing important life skills, and preventing young people from achieving their full potential. The economic wellbeing of young people is defined in *Every Child Matters* as 'not being prevented by economic disadvantage from achieving their full potential in life'. This use of a negative definition (in contrast to the other four themes) indicates that it is harder to identify the positive impact of economic wellbeing than to identify the risks associated with its absence.

The five outcomes themselves are clear:

- children and young people engage in Further education, employment or training on leaving school

- children and young people are ready for employment

- children and young people live in decent homes and sustainable communities

- children and young people have access to transport and material goods

- children and young people live in households free from low income

But their breadth is hugely ambitious. Some, like issues related to low income, material goods and decent housing, are beyond the remit of the average school whose main thrusts are concerned with education, employment and training. Children and Young People's Services and their partners, however, have a responsibility for all outcomes. But the staffing complexities of addressing some of the deeper structural problems associated with disadvantage require the proactive involvement of various agencies such as Connexions, Learning Skills Council, Housing, Early Years Partnership, Neighbourhood Communities and Regeneration, local businesses and development agencies.

Achieve economic wellbeing requires a holistic approach for some of the deep seated issues related to family disadvantage, to patterns of generational unemployment, and to the lack of employability that can have class and cultural origins. For Muslims generally the figures are dire. Over a third live in households with no adults in employment and in almost 75 per cent of Bangladeshi and Pakistani households children live below the poverty line. Over a quarter of 16-24 year old Muslims are unemployed and the majority of Muslim women are economically inactive. It is hardly surprising that Muslim attainment levels are well below national averages. This complex problem requires complex and co-ordinated solutions. As the NYA put it, 'an economic wellbeing agenda must involve interventions at individual, family, community and social levels'.

Schools and Further Education colleges and their business partners concentrate on supporting young people to stay in education, employment or training (EET) and providing them with the basic and higher order skills required for them to access their chosen pathway. For schools and Youth Services it is very much about support and guidance, and about the nurturing of interpersonal and leadership skills.

The Muslim frame of reference supports this theme entirely, for part of the agenda has to be about social justice, about supporting the community in at the widest sense. Muslims, as we have already seen, are 'enjoined' to become fully educated. They are also encouraged to work hard, make money and be successful. For Muslims the issue is not about being involved in trade and commerce, Prophet Muhammad (PBUH) himself was a successful merchant; but it is about being fair and honest in your dealings and about spending your surplus wealth to benefit the poor of the *ummah*, to the ultimate glory of God. 'He who strives on behalf of a widow and a poor person is like one who strives in God's path', argues one *hadith*. Free trade and work are encouraged by the Qur'an when it says 'and when the prayer is finished, then you may disperse through the land, and seek the bounty of God' (62.10). Free trade is permitted as long as it complements fair trade. The Qur'an lays down injunctions that ensure ethical business practices.

There is an on-going debate within the Muslim world about the nature of an Islamic economic system. This is a relatively recent phenomenon, originating in the 1930s. The first Islamic bank started in 1975 but since then a number of western banks have set up their own Islamic branches. Even the Dow Jones has its own Islamic Market, established in 1999, and tracks stocks suitable for Islamic Investors. Islamic economic principles with a Qur'anic basis promote co-operation rather than competition. They favour balance and moderation and discourage lavishness, miserliness and wastefulness.

The major difference between Islamic and Western banking systems, however, relates to taking interest on loans, known as *riba*. The Qur'an explicitly condemns the practice because it can add to the burdens on the poor, and those who are in debt. This prohibition can pose problems for modern Muslims. More banks and mortgage providers are now offering *Shari'ah* compliant personal finance products. Islamic economic principles, like so many other aspects of Islamic thinking, are based upon social and economic justice, a principle that lies at the very heart of achieving economic wellbeing.

Achieve economic wellbeing: questions from Muslim perspectives

- In light of the patterns of unemployment in many Muslim communities, what are you doing to ensure that young Muslims are ready for employment?

- Do you offer careers guidance and counselling that is culturally and religiously sensitive?

- How have you taken the Islamic frame of reference into account when planning your 14-19 curriculum?

- How have you incorporated the Islamic frame of reference when planning your PSHE curriculum?

- How do you know that the 14-19 education and training offered delivers quality outcomes for young Muslims?

- Are you utilising the existing Muslim business links to offer role models, training and support?

- Do you track the engagement of your Muslim pupils in further education, employment and training on leaving school?

- Have you mapped the position of Muslim pupils across all five themes of this outcome? What patterns have emerged and what actions are you taking to address the issues raised?

- Do you have an action plan that particularly targets young Muslim women?

- Do you use the linguistic and cultural backgrounds of your Muslim students to best effect? For example, if your students speak Arabic, Somali, Bengali or Urdu do you exploit these skills?

- Do you offer any particular leadership training for young Muslims?

- Are you aware of the bodies that promote Islamic social enterprise, like Islamic Expo, and the support the Princes Trust offers young Muslims to set up in business?

- Do you offer any training about Islamic ethical principles like Shari'ah compliant banking?

- Do you support young Muslims to *Act by Right* so that they can be involved in making changes happen where they live?

- Do you research, record and celebrate what has changed through the active involvement of young Muslims?

- When you are deciding upon work placements, do you check that they will be sensitive to the needs of Muslim pupils?

- What incentives and support do you offer Muslim employees to become involved in placements, work based training and youth apprentice schemes?

- What career guidance do you offer young Muslims?

- What is the Muslim take-up of study support both online and actually?

- How sensitive is Connexions service to Muslim needs? Do you discuss Muslim issues with them?

- Does your programme for education for sustainable development include Muslim heritage and experiences? Does it make optimal use of the local experiences and the wider Muslim perspectives?

- What is the Muslim take up for child care?

Appendix
Every Muslim Child Matters

Questions for Governors

Whether you are a Muslim or not, a governor of a school with a majority of Muslim pupils, or one where Muslims are in a minority, the issues are essentially the same. It is obviously easier and more cost-effective to cater for Muslim needs when they are in a majority but it is equally, if not more important to make sure that Muslim pupils in a minority feel valued and supported. This guidance, therefore, aims to help all governors meet these needs, and to offer advice to Muslim governors who are not always clear as to their role as Muslims on governing bodies in secular schools.

The first and most important function of governors is that they are the school's 'critical friends'. The key word is friends. There have been some instances where Muslim governors have seen themselves as faith advocates, as an advanced party whose wish is to change the nature of the school from secular to faith. This type of advocacy can cause enormous problems. It can alienate teachers and non-Muslim governors and parents, and might well undermine community cohesion. If Muslim governors want to establish state funded faith schools they should refer to government guidance provided by the School Organising Committee (see the School Organising website, www. dfes.gov.uk/schoolorg/index). This guidance is aimed at governors who wish to ensure that their maintained school meets the needs of its Muslim population.

The second key function of governors is that they are responsible and accountable for the strategic management of the school, and for ensuring that the school meets statutory requirements in areas such as curriculum, race and gender equality, and promoting community cohesion. These are large and complex areas and governors rely upon professional advice and expertise for much of the detailed thinking, and implementation of policy.

Governors need to take informed decisions and the following checklist will help them.

1. Have you an understanding of why faith is so important to Muslims?

2. Do you know how many Muslims there are in your school?

   Schools are not required to collect statistics based on faith so we rely on proxy measures related to ethnicity. The assumption that Bangladeshis, Pakistanis, Somalis and Afghanis are Muslims will be valid. Although Turks and Kurds come from countries where Islam is is practised, it will not necessarily be their main agenda. There are many Muslims from India and care must be taken not to assume that because pupils are of Indian heritage they must be Hindus.

3. Do you know how well your Muslim pupils are doing at each Key Stage?

   You may wish to use this information to offer targeted support.

4. Do you know how many of your Muslim pupils are on the Special Needs Register and the types of need they have?

   There might well be patterns of need and these can be further interrogated with a view to exploring the nature and type of support offered.

5. Is there any evidence of racist incidents, religious intolerance or Islamaphobia? If so, what actions is the school taking to counter these in the short term, and also the longer term by means of the curriculum and cultural issues?

6. How does your school deal with and teach about controversial issues?

   Barely a day passes without some media reference to Islam, often but not always negative and hostile. The problems in Iraq and Afghanistan and the government's drive against extremism ensure that this remains a sensitive issue for Muslim pupils.

7. All the evidence we have demonstrates that effective schools have good and productive links with the parents and communities it serves. What practical steps has your school taken to ensure that Muslim parents feel welcome and are able to discuss sensitive issues with staff? What links, has the school made with its local madrasahs and mosques?

National bodies like the National Resource Centre for Supplementary Education (www.continyou.org.co.uk) and the Leicester Complementary Schools Trust are attempting to link madrasahs and mainstream schools in order to capitalise on the fact that Muslim pupils attend madrasahs out of school time. There are an increasing number of examples where mainstream schools are celebrating pupil achievement gained in the madrasahs.

8. Similarly, evidence indicates that effective schools listen to their pupils, and take action based upon some of these perceptions. Young Muslims can find the world they inhabit very confusing. All the more reason, therefore, to provide them with a platform to hear their views and to provide a teaching environment and culture that helps developing their powers of discussion. Do you as governors hear pupil voice? Do you encourage pupils to articulate their views on all issues, but in particular on issues that relate to their faith?

The views sought might be related to the safer areas of prayer time or diet, but might also be geared to issues related to the nature of the teaching and learning, and the curriculum offered.

9. The quiet curriculum revolution and the increasingly personalised agenda will have a major impact on all schools. Its potential to positively influence the curriculum offered to Muslim pupils is enormous. The advent of the National Curriculum in 1988 signalled the end of debates related to curriculum design and content and the governor's role predominantly became limited to ensuring the National Curriculum was effectively implemented, and to monitor and evaluate the outcomes of their schools curriculum delivery. Pupils were rarely involved in this process. The gradual erosion of central government curriculum prescription provides an ideal opportunity for governors to be involved in curriculum change. This will be of particular value and interest to Muslim governors. The following questions should help to provide a governor framework for curriculum discussions.

- Do you know what curriculum is presently on offer to your pupils?

- What areas of the curriculum lend themselves to the introduction or development of Muslim perspectives?

- Do your Muslim pupils see themselves reflected in your curriculum?

- Has your governing body looked at the QCAs 'Big Picture of the Curriculum'? Have you explored areas of this picture which will support the development of a Muslim identity, for example the focus for learning, the overarching theories, the knowledge and understanding of the world, as well as the traditional national curriculum subjects

- How well do your governors understand the curriculum implications of the Every Muslim Child Matters agenda?

- Has your schools governing body developed twinning links with other schools, especially with those from different faith and cultural backgrounds. What are the curricular implications for school links?

The training implications for these curricular changes will be profound for all schools and their governing bodies. It is unlikely that everyone involved in running schools will have the skill sets required to re-construct a curriculum, especially one that retains a battery of assessments, the result of which are the key public measures by which schools are held accountable. These curriculum discussions provide an ideal opportunity for governors, school leadership teams and schools to become involved in joint training events designed to discuss the wider nature of the curriculum on offer, with special attention to an Islamic frame of relevance.

This debate may not be easy. It will require openness, a degree of sensitivity and empathy and a no-blame culture from all parties, Muslim and non-Muslim, if progress is to be made.

Glossary

Adab	Etiquette
Adhan	The call to prayer before each salah (*ritual prayers*)
Andalous	A musical tradition based in Morocco, preserving the idioms of the period of Muslim rule in Andalucia (Southern Spain)
Asr	Name of prayer offered after mid afternoon
Barelwis	A movement of *Sunni* Islam which began in India
Bismillah	The opening words of the Qur'an meaning 'In the name of God, the Merciful, the Compassionate', often spoken at the start of a new venture. There is a tradition among calligraphers of working these words into the form of a bird
Calligraphy	The art of creating beautiful, often abstract, shapes from the forms of Arabic lettering
Darul-Ulum	'House of knowledge', generally educational institutions, where students study Islamic subjects
Deobandis	Islamic revivalist movement, characterised by strict adherence to the *Sunnah* which began in India
Dervish	A member of a *Sufi* religious fraternity dedicated to poverty, austerity and good works. Traditionally dervishes wandered from place to place, supported by alms
Diaspora	Those members of a cultural, faith or ethnic community who are scattered, away from their homeland
Dhikr	In its broadest sense, the remembrance of God through prayer and reciting the Qur'an. In Sufi usage it denotes repetitive chanting, which may be accompanied by movement, inducing a trance-like state
Fajr	Name of prayer offered before sunrise
Fard	Compulsory duty prescribed by God
Fiqh	Deep understanding – technically in reference to the science of Islamic law
Gamelan	An Indonesian musical tradition featuring metallic percussion, gongs and drums, of Hindu origin. There are two forms, Balinese and Javanese. The Javanese are predominantly Muslim, yet they embrace the cultural forms of gamelan.

161

Ghazal	A poetic form consisting of a loose series of couplets, the last of which sums up the themes of the poem and often invokes the author by name. In Pakistan and India ghazals are a popular song form
Ghusl	The full bath required to enter a state of purity
Hadith	Reported sayings and acts of the Messenger Muhammad (PBUH) and his close companions – *hadith* (singular) *ahadith* (plural)
Hadra	Sufi circling dance
Hafiz	Term used by Muslims for people who have completely memorised the Qur'an
Hajj	Pilgrimage to Makkah
Halal	That which is lawful (permissible) in Islam
Haram	That which is unlawful (forbidden) in Islam
Haya'	Modesty
Hijab	*To cover – primarily refers to woman's head and body being covered,* wider meaning of modesty
Ibadah	Worship of God
Idul-Fitr	Festival marking the end of *Ramadan*
Ihsan	The Muslim responsibility to obtain perfection, or excellence, in worship
Ilm	Knowledge of Islam
Ijma	Refers to the consensus of the ummah
Insha'allah	God Willing
Ijtihad	technical term of Islamic law that describes the process of making a legal decision
Isha'	Name of prayer offered at night time
Izzat	Honour
Jihad	To exercise an effort, to make an effort, to struggle, to strive
Ka'bah	Large cube shaped building located inside the Mosque (Masjidul-Haram) in Makkah, this is the holiest place in Islam
Madinah	Second holiest city in Islam (located in Saudi Arabia) and the burial place of Muhammad (PBUH)
Madrasah	A school for Islamic studies; for UK school children, usually takes the form of after-school classes at the mosque, a major element of which is learning to recite the Qur'an
Maghrib	Name of prayer offered just after Sunset
Makkah	Holiest city in Islam (located in Saudi Arabia), where the *Ka'bah* is located
Masha'allah	God has willed it, all accomplishments are achieved by the will of God – phrase used by Muslims to indicate appreciation
Moghul	The Muslim empire of India
Muhammad	The final messenger of God (PBUH = Peace Be Upon Him)
Mushaira	An informal gathering of friends to read and discuss poetry

Na't	Poems or songs in praise of the Prophet, sung in Urdu – equivalent to *Nasheeds*
Nasheed	Poems or popular songs in praise of the Prophet (PBUH), originally in Arabic, now often in English and other languages
Ottoman	The Muslim empire of the Middle East, ruled from Turkey
Qasidah	A long poem of praise, originating in pre-Islamic Arabia, developed by Persian poets and later giving rise to the *ghazal*
Qawwali	A form of music and poetry developed by Indian Sufis, which has achieved world-wide popularity
Qiblah	The direction to be faced in ritual prayer (*salah*) towards *Ka'bah* in Makkah
Qira'ah	The public recitation of the Qur'an, following closely prescribed rules for pitch, rhythm and tone
Qur'an	Final book of guidance from God, sent down to Prophet Muhammad (PBUH)
Ramadan	9th and holiest month of the Islamic calendar, Muslims are obligated to fast during this month (fourth pillar of Islam)
Riba	Interest, usury
Salah	The second pillar of Islam refers to the five daily prayers, which are compulsory upon all mature Muslims. Each *Salah* is performed facing the *Ka'bah* in Makkah and is offered at fixed times during the day
Sima	Sufi ritual of the Mevlevi dervishes, originally developed by the poet Rumi, which includes the circling dance
Shahadah	The Muslim profession of faith: There is none worthy of worship except God, and Muhammad (PBUH) is his messenger
Shari'ah	Body of Islamic law
Shi'ah	Shi'ah Muslims are the second largest denomination based on the Islamic faith
Sufi	A mystical tradition within Islam, 'a science whose objective is the reparation of the heart and turning it away from all else but God'
Sunnah	The way of the Prophet
Sunni	Sunni Muslims are the largest denomination of Islam
Tahara	Purification, purity
Tajwid	Proper pronunciation, to recite every letter correctly during recitation of the Qur'an
Tariqah	Literally, 'path' or 'way' – the discipline of learning and purification followed by Sufis.
Ulama	Refers to Muslim scholars
Ummah	The united worldwide community of Muslims
Wudu	Ritual ablution that must be made before formal prayer and handling the Qur'an
Zakat	The third pillar of Islam, this is the practice of charitable giving based on accumulated wealth
Zuhr	Name of prayer offered after midday

References

Ali S (1993) *Intellectual Foundations of Muslim Civilization*. Delhi: Al-Amin Publications

Ajegbo K (ed) (2007) *Curriculum Review: Diversity and Citizenship*. London: DfES

Association of Muslim Researchers (1996) *Proceedings of the Conference on Islam and Music: Much Ado About Music*. London: Education Society of the AMR

Billingham C (ed) (2007) *Faith and Education: Responding to school-based issues*. Leicester: Forest Lodge Education Service

Bloom J and Blair S (2000) *Islam: Empire of Faith*. London: BBC Worldwide

Bonney R (2004) *Jihad: The Idea of a Just War from the Qu'ran to Bin Laden*. Hampshire: Palgrave Macmillan

Bukhari, M (1996) *The English Translation of Sahih Al Bukhari: with Arabic text*. Egypt: Al-Saadawi Pubns

Cantle, T (2002) *Community Cohesion: A report of the independent review team*, chaired by Ted Cantle. London: The Home Office

Cassen R and Kingdom G (2007) *Tackling Low Educational Achievement*. York: Joseph Rowntree

Clark K W (2003) *Winning Modern Wars: Iraq, Terrorism and the American Empire*. Public Affairs

Coles M (2005) *Faithful and Proud: Young British Muslims conference report*. Leicester: SDSA

Coles M (2006) *Faith, Interfaith and Cohesion: the Educational Dimension*. Leicester: SDSA and The Institute of Community Cohesion

Coles M and Chilvers P (2004) *Curriculum Reflecting Experiences of African Caribbean and Muslim Pupils*. (CREAM Project) Leicester: SDSA

Coles M and Chilvers P (2004) *Education and Islam: Developing a Culturally Inclusive Curriculum*. Leicester: SDSA

Commission on Integration and Cohesion (2007) *Our Shared Futures*. London: Commission on Integration and Cohesion

Department for Children, Schools and Families (2007) *Guidance on the Duty to Promote Community Cohesion*. London: Department for Children, Schools and Families

Department for Children, Schools and Families (2007) *Ethnicity and Education: The evidence on minority ethnic pupils aged 3-16*. London: DCSF

Department for Communities and Local Government (2007) *Preventing Violent Extremism – Winning Hearts and Minds*. London: DCSF

Department for Education and Skills (2001) *Tomorrow's Future: Building a Strategy for Children and Young People*. London: DfES

Department for Education and Skills (2003) *Every Child Matters: Green Paper*. Norwich: TSO

Department for Education and Skills (2005) *Hear by Right*. London: DfES

Department for Education and Skills (2005) *Youth Matters*. London: DfES

Department for Education and Skills (2006) *Ethnicity and Education: The Evidence on Minority Ethnic Pupils Aged 5-16*. London: DfES

Department for Education and Skills (2007) *Every Parent Matters*. London: DfES

el Fadl K A (2007) *The Great Theft: Wrestling Islam from the Extremists*. New York: Harper Collins

European Monitoring Centre on Racism and Xenophobia (2002) Islamophobia in the EU after September 11th 2001. Austria: European Monitoring Centre

The Federation of Student Islamic Societies in the UK and Eire (FOSIS) (2005) *The Muslim Student Survey*. FOSIS: London

Fullan M (2001) *Leading in a Culture of Change*. Sussex: Jossey-Bass

Gilbert, C (2006) *The Annual Report of Her Majesty's Chief Inspector of Schools 2005/06*. London: Ofsted http://www.ofsted.gov.uk/publications/20060008 (August 2007)

Gohir S (2007) Concerns over GP Confidentiality Breaches. *Islamic Times* www.islamictimes.co. uk/content/view/662/50/

Goody, J and Thomas K (2004) *Multicultural Literature in the Classroom: Teacher account of innovative work with years 5-12*. Sheffield: National Association for the Teaching of English (NATE) (www.nate.org)

Hafez S (ed) (2003) *Safe Children, Sound Learning: Guidance for Madressahs*. Kirklees: Kirklees Education/Social Services

al-Hassani S T S (ed) (2006) *1001 Inventions: Muslim Heritage in our world*. Manchester: Foundation for Science Technology and Civilization (FSTC)

Haw K (1998) *Educating Muslim Girls: Shifting Discourses*. Buckingham: Open University Press

Huntington S (2002) *Clash of Civilisations and the Remaking of World Order*. London: Free Press

Hussain E (2007) *The Islamist: Why I Joined Radical Islam in Britain: What I Saw Inside and Why I Left*. London: Penguin Books

Jones G (2007) *The Implications for Youth Work of Every Child Matters: Theme 5: Economic wellbeing*. Leicester: National Youth Agency

Meddeb A (2003) *Islam and its Discontents*. London: William Heinemann

Minority Ethnic Achievement Project (2007) *Raising the Achievement of Pakistani, Bangladeshi, Somali and Turkish heritage pupils: a management guide*. London: DfES

Muslim Council of Britain (2002) *The Quest for Sanity – Reflections on September 11th and the Aftermath*. London: Muslim Council of Britain

Muslim Council of Britain (2007) *Towards Greater Understanding: meeting the needs of Muslim pupils in state schools*. London: Muslim Council of Britain

Muslim Liaison Committee (1999) *Guidelines on Meeting the Religious and Cultural Needs of Muslims*. London: Muslim Liaison Committee and Birmingham City Council

Newham Emds and Mantra Lingua (2007) *Developing a Culturally Inclusive Curriculum* (info@ mantralingua.com)

Ostberg, S (2006) *Islamic Nurture and Identity Management: the lifeworld of Muslim children and young people in Norway*. Netherlands: Springer

Parekh, B (2005) *The Future of Multi-Ethnic Britain*. London: Profile Books

Qualification and Curriculum Association (2007) *The New Secondary Curriculum: What has Changed and Why*. London: QCA

Ramadan T (1994) *To be a European Muslim*. Leicester: The Islamic Foundation

Ramadan T (2004) *Western Muslims and the Future of Islam.* New York: Oxford University Press

Ramadan T (2007) *The Messenger: The Meanings of the Life of Muhammad (PBUH).* London: Allen Lane

Raza M S (1991) *Islam in Britain: Past, Present and Future.* Leicester: Volcano Press

Richardson R (ed) (1997) *Islamophobia: A Challenge for Us All.* London: The Runnymede Trust

Richardson R (ed) (2004) *Islamophobia: Issues, Challenges and Action – A Report by the Commission on British Muslims and Islamophobia.* Stoke on Trent: Trentham Books

Richardson R and Wood A (2004) *The Achievement of British Pakistani Learners: Work in Progress.* (RAISE Project). Stoke on Trent: Trentham Books

Seddon M S, Hussain D and Malik N (2003) *British Muslims: Loyalty and Belonging.* Leicester: Islamic Foundation:

Shahid Dr (2004) *Sickening State of Muslim Health in Britain.* London: Muslim Council of Britain

Shain F (2003) *The Schooling and Identity of Asian Girls.* Stoke on Trent: Trentham Books

Siddiqui, A (2007) *Islam at Universities in England: meeting the needs and investing in the future.* London: DfES

Vincent, R (2007) Intervene to Succeed: using education data to raise achievement for pupils of minority ethnic origin. (*Race Equality Teaching* 25.2 Spring)

Websites

1001 Inventions
www.1001inventions.com(August 2007)

BBC news (2005) 7 July bomber 'filmed last year.' Mohammed Sidique Khan
http://news.bbc.co.uk/1/hi/uk/4375598.stm (August 2007)

Binyon, M (2007) Poll reveals Muslims as model citizens
http://www.timesonline.co.uk/tol/news/uk/article1662695.ece (August 2007)

Black Information Link
www.blink.org.uk (August 2007)

Black Radley Limited
www.blackradley.com (August 2007)

Bradford Schools
www.bradfordschools.net (August 2007)

Burke, J (2003) The Bush Beater.
http://books.guardian.co.uk/reviews/politicsphilosophyandsociety/0,,1091064,00.html (August 2007)

Butt, H (2007) Article II. My plea to fellow Muslims: you must renounce terror.
www.guardian.co.uk/commentisfree/story/0,,2115891,00.html (August 2007)

Christian Muslim Forum
www.christianmuslimforum.org (August 2007)

Department for Work and Pensions
www.dwp.gov.uk/ (August 2007)

EMEL – *The Muslim Lifestyle Magazine*
www.emel.com (August 2007)

Foster Care Link
www.fostercarelink.com (August 2007)

Gallup World Poll
www.gallupworldpoll.com (August 2007)

Howe, D Who you calling a nigger? Channel 4
www.channel4.com (August 2007)

Inservice Training and Educational Development
http://www.insted.co.uk/ (August 2007)

Institute of Community Cohesion
www.coventry.ac.uk/icoco/a/264

Islam and Citizenship Education (ICE)
www.theiceproject.com

Jones, G (2007) *Economic Wellbeing: the implications of youth work for Every Child Matters*
http://www.nya.org.uk/shared_asp_files/uploadedfiles/2c9b0903-fb76-4f93-8854-
1380f5c0e586_economicwellbeing.pdf (August 2007)

The Local Government Association (2002) *Guidance on Community Cohesion.*
http://www.lga.gov.uk/Publication.asp?1section=59&id=-A7814115 (August 2007)

Muslim Health Network
www.muslimhealthnetwork.org (August 2007)

Muslim Youth Helpline
www.myh.org.uk/services.php?id=4 Ramadan Behind Bars Campaign (September 2007)

Muslim Voice
www.mvuk.co.uk (August 2007)

Nasiha – practical citizenship
www.nasiha.co.uk (August 2007)

National Foundation for Education Research
www.nfer.ac.uk/index.cfm (August 2007)

National Statistics
www.statistics.gov.uk (August 2007)

NCSL and Becta Matrix
http://matrix.becta.org.uk (August 2007)

QCA
www.qca.org.uk (August 2007)

Futures – meeting the challenge
www.qca.org.uk/futures (August 2007)

Futures in action: building a 21st Century Curriculum
www.qca.org.uk/futuresinaction (August 2007)

National Framework for Religious Education
www.qca.org.uk/qca_7886.aspx (August 2007)

A Big Picture of the Curriculum
http://www.qca.org.uk/qca_5856.aspx (August 2007)

Raban, J (2003) *The Greatest Gulf.*
http://books.guardian.co.uk/departments/politicsphilosophyandsociety/story/0,,939435,00.html
(August 2007)

The Radical Middle Way Project
www.radicalmiddleway.co.uk (August 2007)

The Russell Commission
www.archivecabinetoffice.gov.uk/russellcommission

Salaam
www.salaam.co.uk (August 2007)

REFERENCES

School Development Support Agency (SDSA)
CREAM project and FAME project
www.sdsa.net (August 2007)

Spalek, B (2005) Muslims in British Prisons
http://www.hmprisonservice.gov.uk/assets/documents/100011E4496_muslims_in_british_prisons.doc (August 2007)

Supplementary Schools Network
www.supplementaryschools.org.uk (August 2007)

Ward, H and Bloom, A (2007) Creativity back in favour. *TES*
http://www.tes.co.uk/search/story/?story_id=2394568 (August 2007)

Zaytuna Institute and Academy
http://www.zaytuna.org/ (August 2007)

Index